· TROPHIES ·

Practice Book

Grade 1 ◆ Volume Two

Harcourt

Orlando   Boston   Dallas   Chicago   San Diego

Visit *The Learning Site!*
www.harcourtschool.com

ISBN-13: 978-0-15-323505-4   ISBN-10: 0-15-323505-5

34 0982 13 12

4500370803

Contents

TIME TOGETHER – THEME 5

Contents

TIME TOGETHER – THEME 5

Contents

GATHER AROUND – THEME 6

Contents

GATHER AROUND – THEME 6

Name _____

▶ **Read the chart. Then write the contraction that completes each sentence.**

She is	She's
he is	he's
do not	don't
can not	can't
I will	I'll

_____
- - - - - - - - - - -

1. Kate is tired. _____ going to bed.

_____
- - - - - - - - - - -

2. The cat can purr, but it _____ bark.

_____
- - - - - - - - - - -

3. I want some cake. _____ make it.

_____
- - - - - - - - - - -

4. Jack is late, but _____ on his way.

_____
- - - - - - - - - - -

5. I _____ have a red hat.

© Harcourt

SCHOOL-HOME CONNECTION Read the sentences with your child. Discuss item number 1. Ask your child to identify who is meant by the word *she's*. Discuss the word *he's* in number four.

39

Name _____

▶ **Read the words. Then read the name of each group. Write each word in the group where it belongs.**

Words With <u>i-e</u>

_____

_____

_____

_____

_____

_____

_____

_____

Words With <u>a-e</u>

_____

_____

_____

_____

_____

Word With <u>y</u>

_____

_____

Word With <u>o</u>

_____

_____

Spelling Words

ice

nice

rice

race

face

space

like

nine

why

most

SCHOOL-HOME CONNECTION Read the Spelling Words with your child. Make a list of words that rhyme with the Spelling Words. Then make up silly sentences using two or more rhyming words.

40

© Harcourt

Practice Book
Time Together • Lesson 5

Name _____

▶ **Write the word that best completes each sentence.**

| ~~city~~ | ~~space~~ | ~~ice~~ | ~~mice~~ | ~~nice~~ |

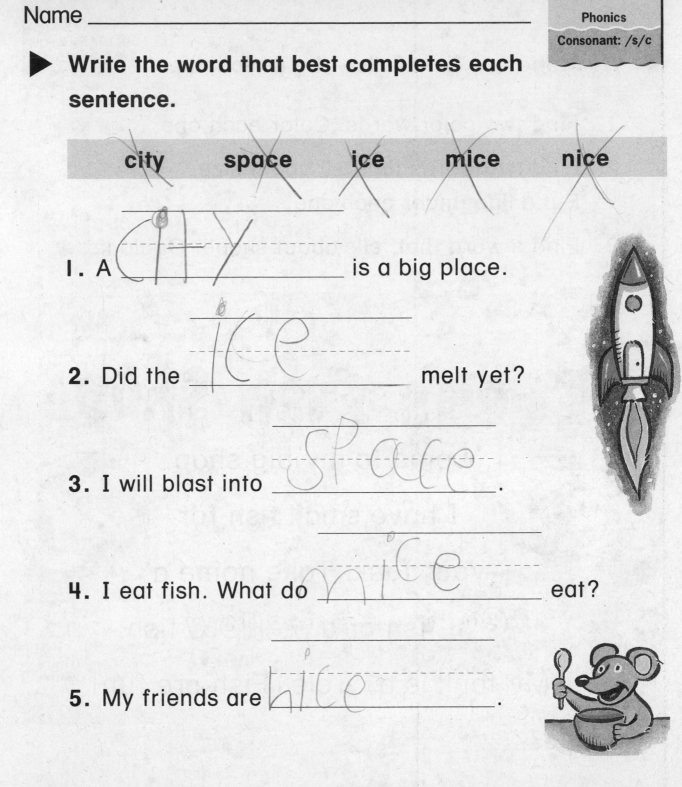

1. A _____city_____ is a big place.

2. Did the ___ice___ melt yet?

3. I will blast into ___space___.

4. I eat fish. What do ___mice___ eat?

5. My friends are ___nice___.

TRY THIS Fold a piece of paper into four squares. Use four words from the box. Write one word on each square and draw a picture about each word.

SCHOOL-HOME CONNECTION Write the word *space*. Talk about the sound that *s* and *c* stand for. With your child, circle all the letters on the page that stand for the sound /s/.

Practice Book
Time Together • Lesson 5

Name _____

► **Read the ad. Then follow the directions.**

1. Find two color words. Color each one.

2. Find two words that tell about size.
   Put a line under each one.

3. Find a word that tells about shape. Circle it.

Fred's Fish Shop

Come to my big shop.

I have small fish for

your tank. Take home a

red fish or a **yellow** fish.

My tank is a circle. Fish are fun!

TRY THIS Look around the classroom. Draw something you see. Write four describing words about it. Use words that tell about size, shape, and color.

SCHOOL-HOME CONNECTION Make a chart with three columns, one for color words, one for size words, and one for shape words. With your child, add words to each column.

Practice Book
Time Together • Lesson 5

© Harcourt

▶ **Write the word from the box that best matches each clue.**

race	face	dance	mice	nice

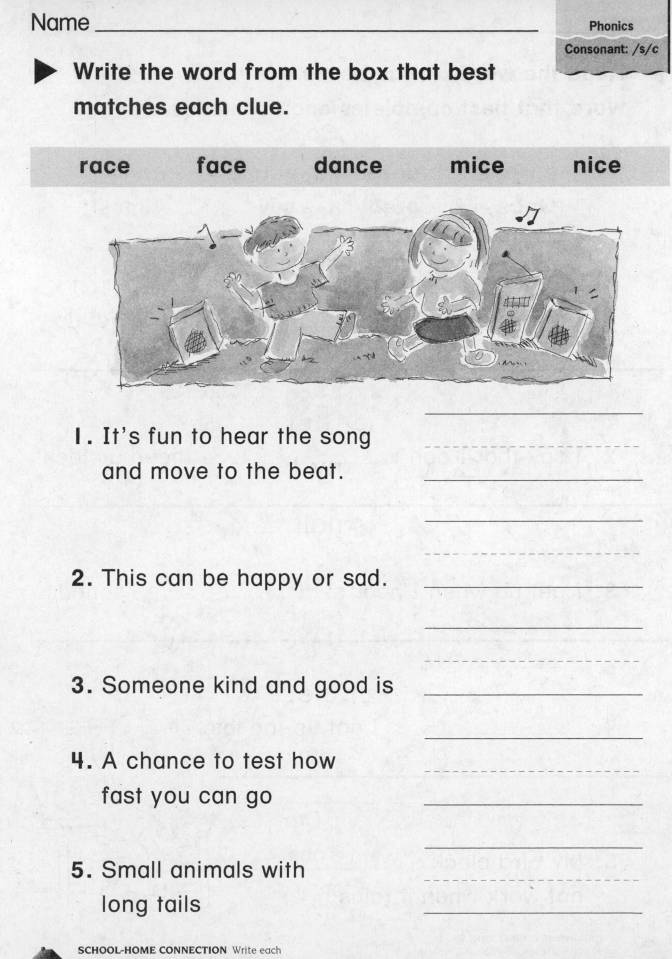

1. It's fun to hear the song and move to the beat.

_____

2. This can be happy or sad.

_____

3. Someone kind and good is

_____

4. A chance to test how fast you can go

_____

5. Small animals with long tails

_____

SCHOOL-HOME CONNECTION Write each word on a card. Have your child match the rhyming words. Take turns using the words in sentences.

43

© Harcourt

Name _____

▶ **Read the words in the box. Write the word that best completes each sentence.**

always	does	sound	even
Once	pretty	say	Almost

_____

1. I almost _____ know when to get up.

_____

2. I say that I don't _____ need a clock!

_____

3. I get up when I hear a _____ sound.

_____

4. _____ I got up too late.

_____

5. My bird clock _____ not work when it rains.

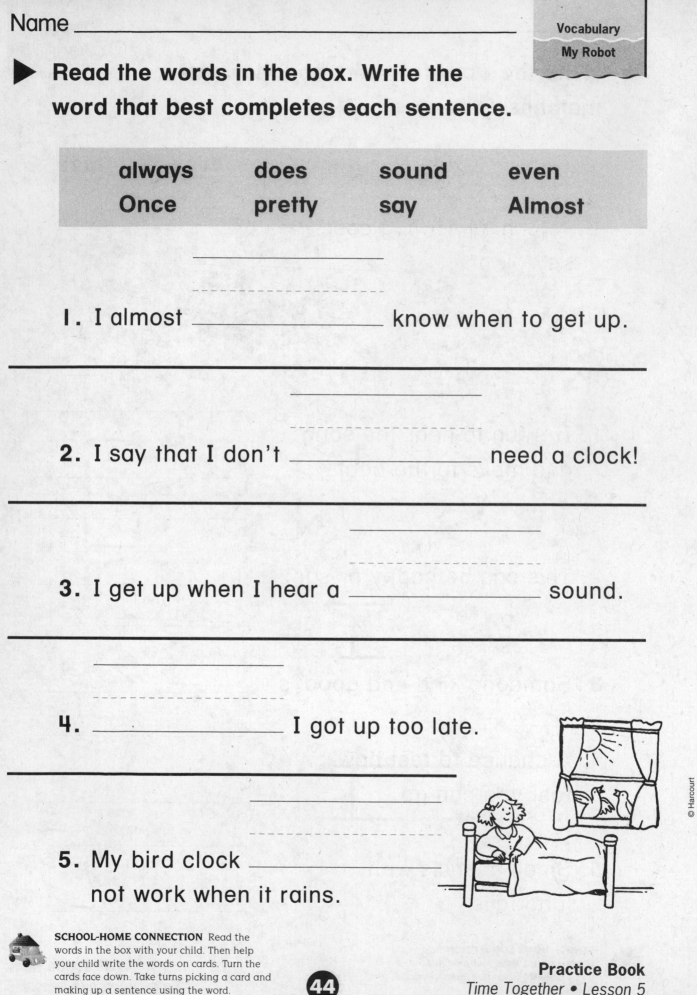

SCHOOL-HOME CONNECTION Read the words in the box with your child. Then help your child write the words on cards. Turn the cards face down. Take turns picking a card and making up a sentence using the word.

Practice Book
Time Together • Lesson 5

Name _____

▶ **Write the words where they belong in the puzzle.**

| spice | price | laces | mice | place | slice |

1. how much something costs
2. where you are

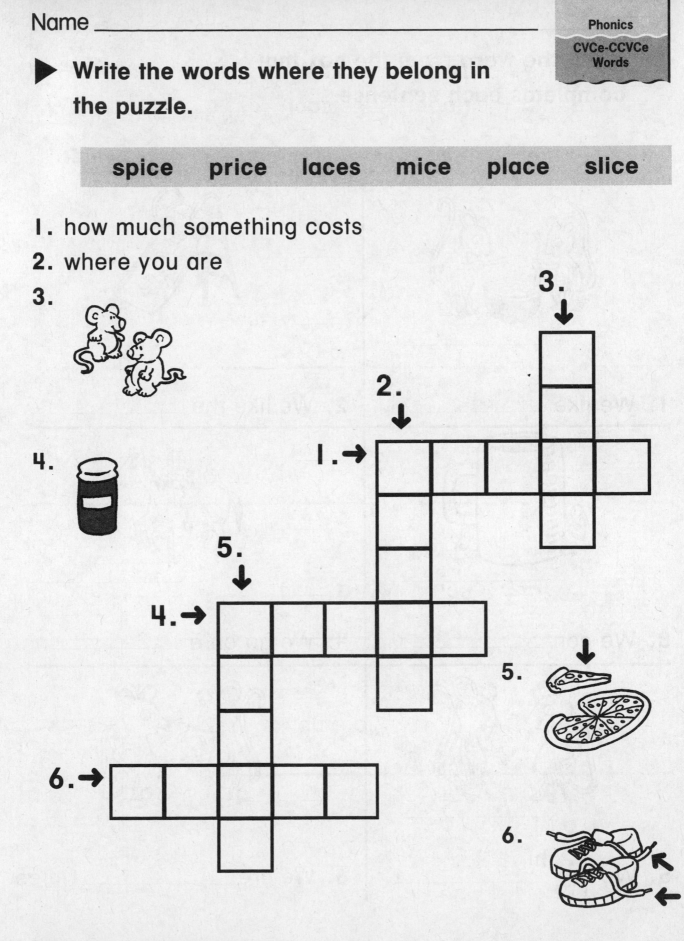

3.

4.

5.

6.

SCHOOL-HOME CONNECTION Read the words in the box with your child. Have your child write a rhyming word for each word in the puzzle.

45

Practice Book
Time Together • Lesson 5

© Harcourt

Name _____

▶ **Write the word from the box that completes each sentence.**

| nice | ride | hide | mice | slide | rice |

1. We like _____.

2. We like the _____.

3. We can _____.

4. We go on a _____.

5. We are _____.

6. We are _____ mice.

SCHOOL-HOME CONNECTION Ask your child to separate the words in the box into two groups. Take turns saying pairs of rhyming words.

Practice Book
Time Together • Lesson 5

© Harcourt

Name _____

▶ **Read the words. Then read the name of each group. Write each word in the group where it belongs.**

Words With <u>ow</u>

_____   _____
_____   _____
_____   _____

Words With <u>ou</u>

_____   _____
_____   _____

Words Without <u>ow</u> or <u>ou</u>

_____   _____
_____   _____
_____   _____

Spelling Words

cow
how
now
down
out
round
nice
face
does
once

© Harcourt

SCHOOL-HOME CONNECTION Read the
Spelling Words with your child. Draw a picture
based on the words in the list. Help your child
write a sentence to go with your picture.

 47

Practice Book
Time Together • Lesson 6

Name _____

▶ **Read each sentence. Draw a line under the words with the /ou/ sound as in <u>out</u>. Then draw a picture to go with each sentence.**

1. The mouse king

has a crown.

2. The clown is

under a cloud.

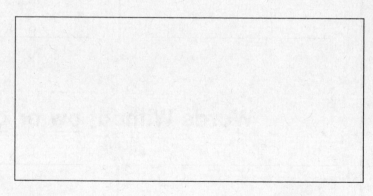

3. The hound dog

found a ball.

4. Mrs. Down's

house is brown.

 SCHOOL-HOME CONNECTION Fold a piece of paper in half the long way. Write *ow* and *ou* at the top of each side. Have your child write words with *ow* and *ou* in the columns. Read the words together.

© Harcourt

Name _____

▶ **Read the chart. Write the word from the chart that best completes each sentence.**

Taste words	Smell words	Sound words	Feel words
sweet	fresh	loud	hard
sour	rotten	soft	fluffy

1. _____ are _____.

2. A _____ is _____.

3. A _____ is _____.

4. Hot _____ smells _____.

5. A _____ can be _____.

 SCHOOL-HOME CONNECTION Add one more word to each category in the chart on this page. Think of something that represents the new describing word.

 49

Practice Book
Time Together • Lesson 6

▶ **Read the story. Circle the words with <u>ow</u>.**
Draw a line under the words with <u>ou</u>. Write all the
words in the chart. Write each word just one time.

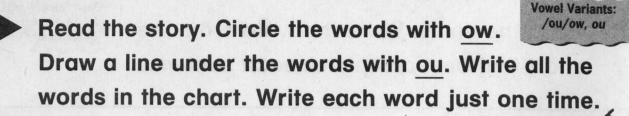

The mouse came back from town.

"How are you?" she said.

"I found a crown," said the cow.

"Where is my crown?" growled the hound dog.

The mouse and cow bowed. The king put on his crown.

ou	**ow**

SCHOOL-HOME CONNECTION Ask your child
to read the story to you. Together, think of
other words with the sound /ou/ as in *loud* and
down.

Practice Book
Time Together • Lesson 6

© Harcourt

Name _____

▶ **Read the words in the box. Write the word that best completes each sentence.**

any	busy	care	Dr.	eight	took

_____

1. Dr. Lee is always very _____.

_____

2. She takes _____ of animals.

_____

3. She _____ care of my dog.

_____

4. She took care of my _____ fish.

_____

5. She can help _____ animal.

SCHOOL-HOME CONNECTION Talk with your child about the doctors your family sees. Write their names on a piece of paper. Have your child write the word *Dr.* for each one.

51

Practice Book
Time Together • Lesson 6

© Harcourt

Name _____

▶ **Read each clue. Write a word from the box that tells about the clue.**

crown	cloud	growl	shout	clown

1.  Look up outside. You might see this. _cloud_

2. This is a hat for a queen. _crown_

3. This man is funny. _clown_

4. This sound is loud. _shout_

5. A dog might do this. _growl_

SCHOOL-HOME CONNECTION Have your child read the words he or she wrote. Then ask him or her to circle the words that rhyme (*clown, crown*).

52

Practice Book
Time Together • Lesson 6

Name _____

▶ **Read the words in the box. Read the headings. Write each word in the correct group. Then add one more thing to each group.**

| apple | beet | letter | note | sandwich | story |

Things to Eat

_____

_____

_____

_____

_____

_____

_____

Things to Read

_____

_____

_____

_____

_____

_____

_____

SCHOOL-HOME CONNECTION Ask your child to read aloud the lists he or she wrote. Together, think of other things to add to each list.

53

© Harcourt

Name _____

▶ **Read each clue. Write the words from the box where they belong in the puzzle.**

| down | brown | town | round | mound | found |

1. A baseball pitcher stands on this.
2. A color
3. The shape of a ball
4. A place with streets, houses, and shops
5. Up and _____
6. Lost and _____

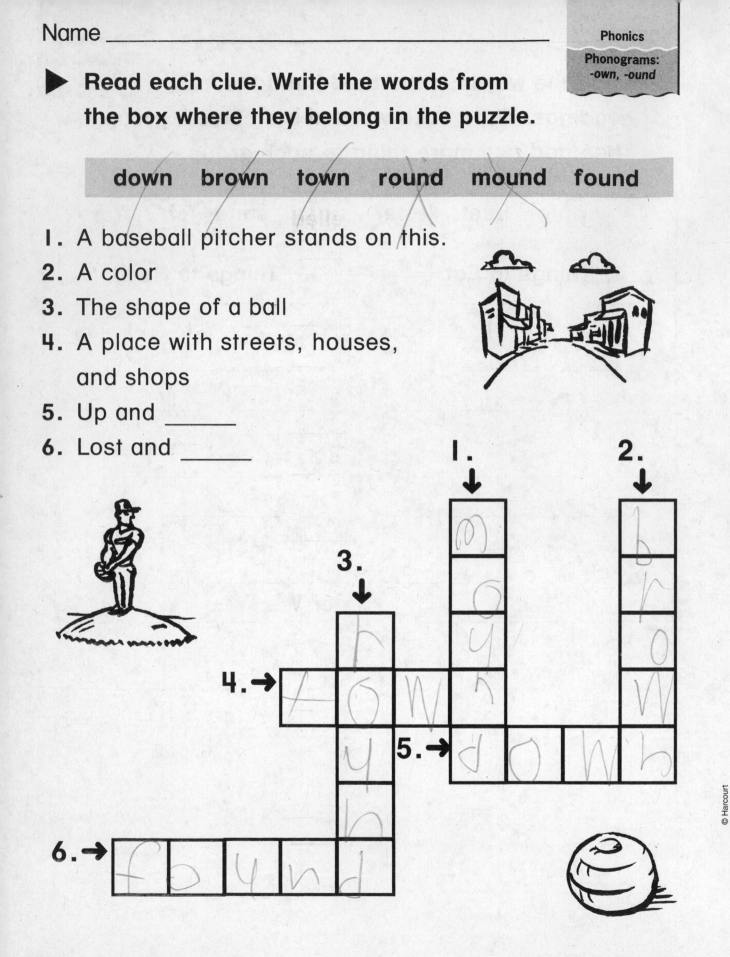

 SCHOOL-HOME CONNECTION Ask your child to name two more words that rhyme with *town* and *found*.

54

Practice Book
Time Together • Lesson 6

© Harcourt

Name _____

▶ **Read the words. Then read the name of each group. Write each word in the group where it belongs.**

Words With Long i Spelled y

_____

_____

_____

_____

_____

_____

_____

_____

_____

_____

Words With ou and ow

_____

_____

_____

Other Words

_____

_____

_____

Spelling Words

my
fly
by
why
sky
try
out
now
any
eight

SCHOOL-HOME CONNECTION Ask your child to read the Spelling Words aloud. Ask your child what he or she will do to remember the spellings.

55

Practice Book
Time Together • Lesson 7

© Harcourt

▶ **Read the story. Write the word or words that best complete the sentence.**

sky	cry	fly	Why	try	tie

1. "_____ do you _____?"

   Toad asked.

2. "Because I can't _____ to my nest," said Owl.

3. "I need to get into the _____, but I can't

   get my _____ out."

4. "I will _____ to help,"

   said Toad.

© Harcourt

SCHOOL-HOME CONNECTION With your child, use the words in the box to write a rhyme about Owl and Toad.

56

Practice Book
Time Together • Lesson 7

Name _____

▶ **Read the sentences. Each sentence tells
how many. Circle the word that tells how
many. Then color how many Teddy got.**

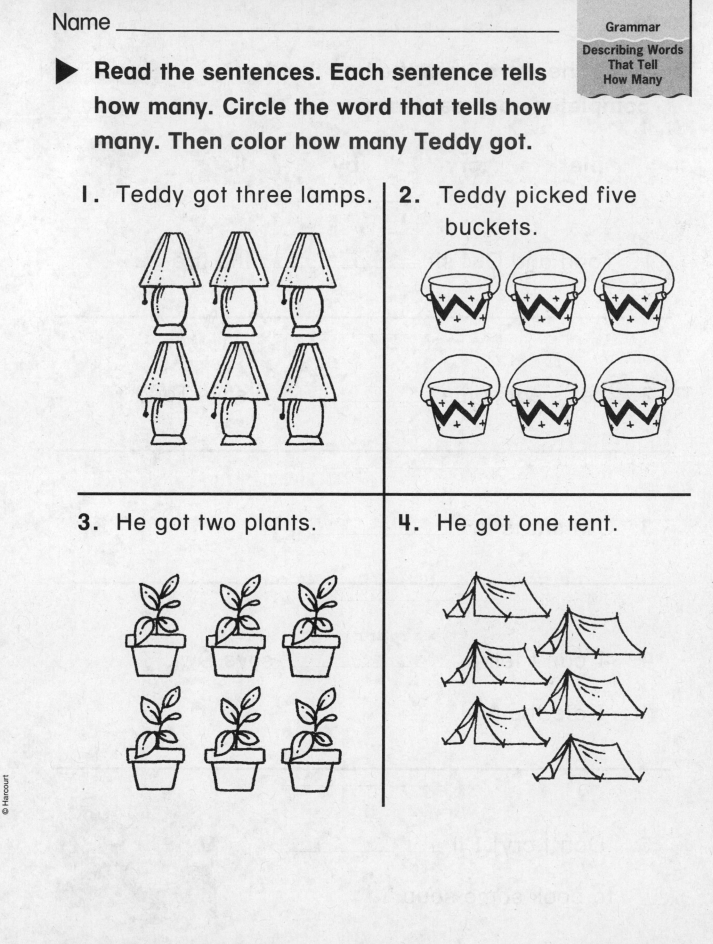

1. Teddy got three lamps.

2. Teddy picked five buckets.

3. He got two plants.

4. He got one tent.

SCHOOL-HOME CONNECTION Ask your
child how many plants and lamps Teddy
bought altogether. Help him or her write an
addition sentence that tells how many.

Practice Book
Time Together • Lesson 7

▶ **Write the word from the box that best completes each sentence.**

pie	cry	by	lie	try

1. Toad and Owl sit _____ the fire.

2. "Let's eat some _____," says Toad.

3. Owl starts to _____.

4. "I can't tell a _____," says Owl.

"I ate the pie!"

5. "Don't cry! I'll _____

to cook some soup."

SCHOOL-HOME CONNECTION Work with your child to write three sentences that use the word *by*.

58

Practice Book
Time Together • Lesson 7

© Harcourt

▶ **Write the word that best completes each sentence.**

| again | blue | High | love | opened | Hello |

_____

1. "_____, Betsy. It's me, Jill."

_____

_____

2. "Hi Jill. Can you bring my _____ bag to school? I left it at your house again."

_____

3. "OK," said Jill. "Did you know a new ice cream

_____

shop _____?"

_____

_____

4. "No! I _____ ice cream! Where is it?"

_____

_____

5. "It's on _____ Street. Let's go after school!"

SCHOOL–HOME CONNECTION Have your child retell the phone conversation in his or her own words. Ask your child to say other sentences that use the words in the box.

59

Practice Book
Time Together • Lesson 7

© Harcourt

Name _____

► **Write a word from the box to complete each sentence.**

| fly | sandy | windy | sky | jelly |

1. The sun is out.

_____

The _____ is blue.

_____

----

2. Birds _____ high above us.

_____

----

3. It's getting pretty _____!

_____

----

4. Gus wants his _____ sandwich.

_____

----

5. We are all _____ when we leave.

SCHOOL-HOME CONNECTION Have your child read the words in the box. Then ask your child to think of other words that rhyme with *sky*. Help your child write the new words.

60

Practice Book
Time Together • Lesson 7

© Harcourt

Name _____

► Tess and Dan are at ABC Farm. The animals at this farm are in ABC order. Write the names of the animals Tess and Dan see as they walk through ABC Farm.

| frog | pig | horse |
| mouse | cow | duck |

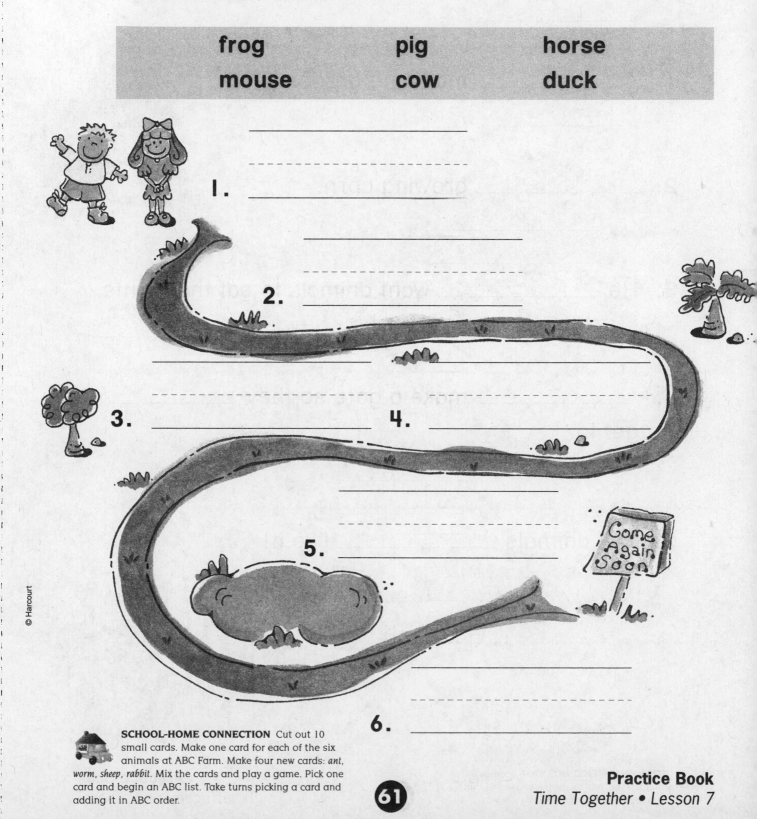

1. _____

2. _____

3. _____

4. _____

5. _____

6. _____

SCHOOL-HOME CONNECTION Cut out 10 small cards. Make one card for each of the six animals at ABC Farm. Make four new cards: *ant, worm, sheep, rabbit.* Mix the cards and play a game. Pick one card and begin an ABC list. Take turns picking a card and adding it in ABC order.

61

Practice Book
Time Together • Lesson 7

© Harcourt

Name _____

▶ **Use a contraction to complete each sentence.**

don't	can't	doesn't	Jack's	He's	He'll

_____

- - - - - - - - -

1. _____ making a garden.

_____

- - - - - - - - -

2. _____ growing corn.

_____

- - - - - - - - -

3. He _____ want animals to eat the plants.

_____   _____

- - - - - - - - -   - - - - - - - - -

4. _____ make a gate so they _____
get in.

_____

- - - - - - - - -

5. The animals _____ like it!

SCHOOL-HOME CONNECTION Review the
contractions. Talk about the two words that
make up each contraction.

62

Practice Book
Time Together • Lesson 7

© Harcourt

► **Read the words. Then read the name of each group. Write each word in the group where it belongs.**

Words With <u>o-e</u>

_____   _____

_____   _____

_____   _____

_____   _____

_____   _____

_____   _____

Words With <u>y</u>   **Words Without <u>o</u> or <u>y</u>**

_____   _____

_____   _____

_____   _____

_____   _____

Spelling Words

bone
cone
code
rode
rose
those
my
try
again
blue

SCHOOL-HOME CONNECTION Ask your child to read the Spelling Words to you. Then write these words on a piece of paper: *cane, ride, rise, these, me.* Have your child change one letter in each to make a Spelling Word.

63

Name _____

▶ **Write the word that best completes each sentence in the story.**

home	nose	hole	stove	bone	mole

_____

1. This is a _____ in the dirt.

_____

2. It is the door to my _____.

_____

3. You see, I am a _____.

_____

4. I sniff with my _____.

_____

5. I have a _____.

_____

6. I will make soup with this _____.

SCHOOL-HOME CONNECTION Use the phonograms *-ole* and *-one* to form more words with long vowel *o*.

64

© Harcourt

Name _____

▶ **Read the chart. Then write the word that best completes each sentence.**

| sunny | rainy | snowy | stormy | cloudy |

1. It is a _____ day.

2. It is a _____ day.

3. It is a _____ day.

4. It is a _____ day.

 TRY THIS Write a story about today's weather.

SCHOOL-HOME CONNECTION Together, read the weather report in a newspaper. Help your child find words that describe the weather.

 65

© Harcourt

▶ **Read the words. Write the word that finishes each sentence.**

| bone | home | pole | robe | woke |

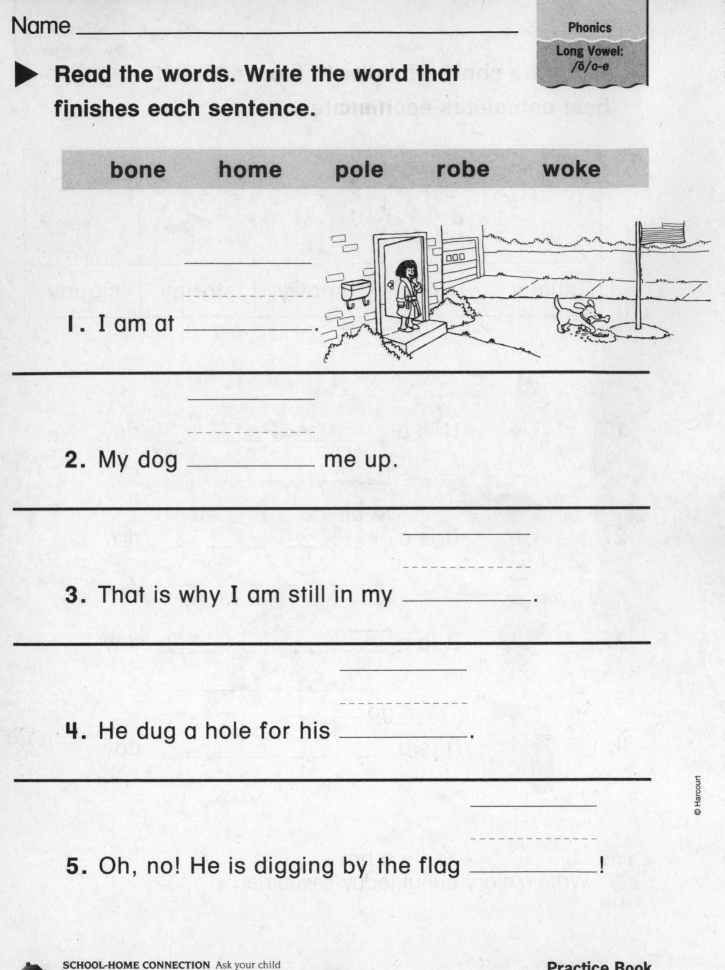

_____

1. I am at _____.

_____

2. My dog _____ me up.

_____

3. That is why I am still in my _____.

_____

4. He dug a hole for his _____.

_____

5. Oh, no! He is digging by the flag _____!

SCHOOL-HOME CONNECTION Ask your child to read aloud the sentences. Discuss what is the same about the words he or she wrote.

66

Practice Book
Time Together • Lesson 8

Name _____

▶ **Write the word from the box that best completes each sentence.**

| another | wait | change | field | touch | wild | twelve |

_____

1. Pa Bear baked _____ apple pies.

2. "Wait! Do not _____ the hot pies," he said.

3. Pa bear said, "No wild play in the house.

   Go be wild in the _____ ".

4. Then Pa said, "Now go _____ your shirts."

5. "Yum! May we please have _____ ?" they said.

SCHOOL-HOME CONNECTION Have your child read aloud the words in the box. Write each word on a separate slip of paper. Turn them over. Take turns picking a card and saying a sentence that uses the word.

Practice Book
Time Together • Lesson 8

► **Write the words from the box where they belong in the puzzle.**

| cot | box | nose | note | rose | sob |

1. a flower
2. something you write
3. part of your face
4. cry
5. a small bed
6. you can put things in this

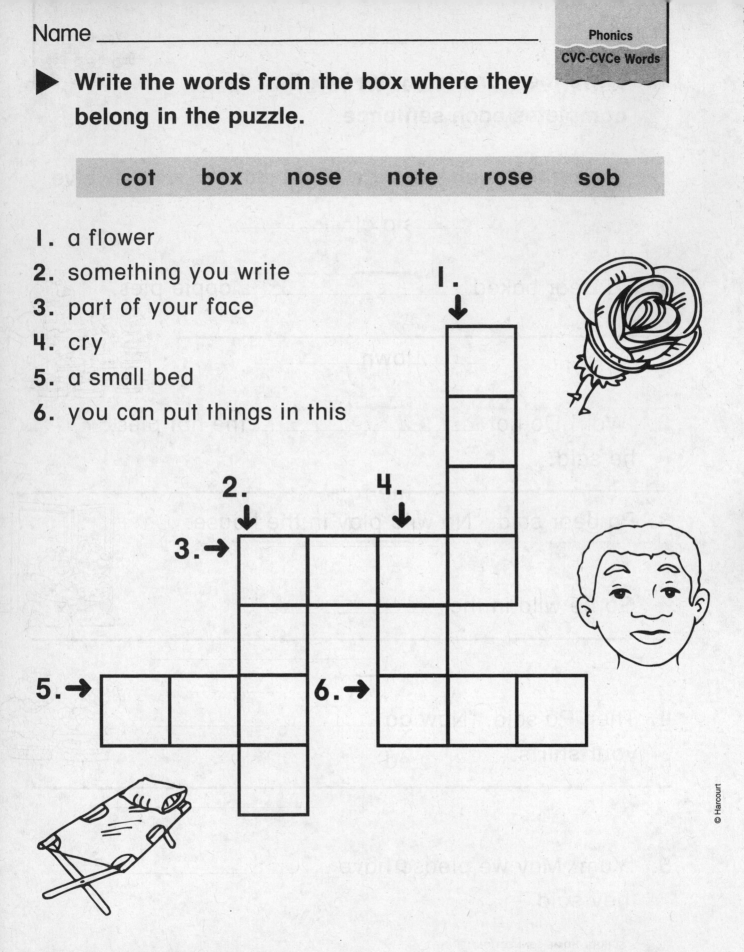

SCHOOL-HOME CONNECTION Read the
words in the box with your child. Talk about the
different vowel sounds with and without the
final *e*.

68

Practice Book
Time Together • Lesson 8

© Harcourt

Name _____

▶ **Read each sentence. Write <u>cl</u>, <u>gl</u>, or <u>sl</u> to finish each word.**

1. The _____own drinks a glass of milk.

2. He is a _____eepy clown.

3. He is _____ad it is time for bed.

4. He _____ips on his _____ippers.

5. He _____imbs into bed

and goes to _____eep.

© Harcourt

Patch's Treat

1

This cat will do anything for fun!
Those feet look like socks.

3

© Harcourt

Let's go home, Patch. You need
a treat. I'll feed you.

8

Please, Dad, can I keep him?
I'll also clean my room for him.

6

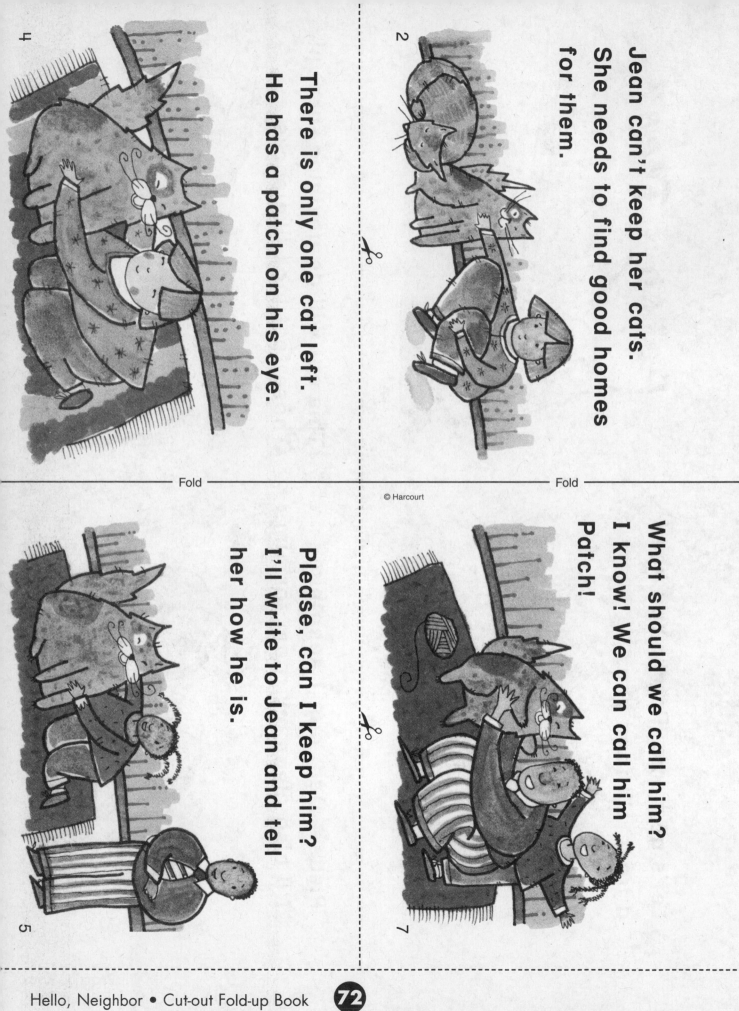

4

There is only one cat left.
He has a patch on his eye.

2

Jean can't keep her cats.
She needs to find good homes
for them.

© Harcourt

5

Please, can I keep him?
I'll write to Jean and tell
her how he is.

7

What should we call him?
I know! We can call him
Patch!

1

Baseball!

3

8

People like
to watch the
players step
up to the plate
and hit the ball.
CRACK!

6

Children in many
countries play the game.
They play in the same way—
with a ball, a bat, and a mitt.

© Harcourt

Fold

Fold

4

The game was
first played
in the United
States of America.
It was called
"town ball." Later it
became baseball.

5

2

Baseball is played all over the
world. It doesn't take much to play
the game. You need a ball, a bat,
some mitts, and a big place to play.

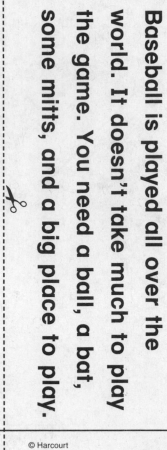

© Harcourt

Fold

7

Eating Yummy Cake

1

I would like a different kind of cake. Do you have Sticky Cake?

3

I had this when I was four years old! Patty Cake is the best!

8

Hold on. I have a cake that is still warm from the oven.

6

Fold

Fold

© Harcourt

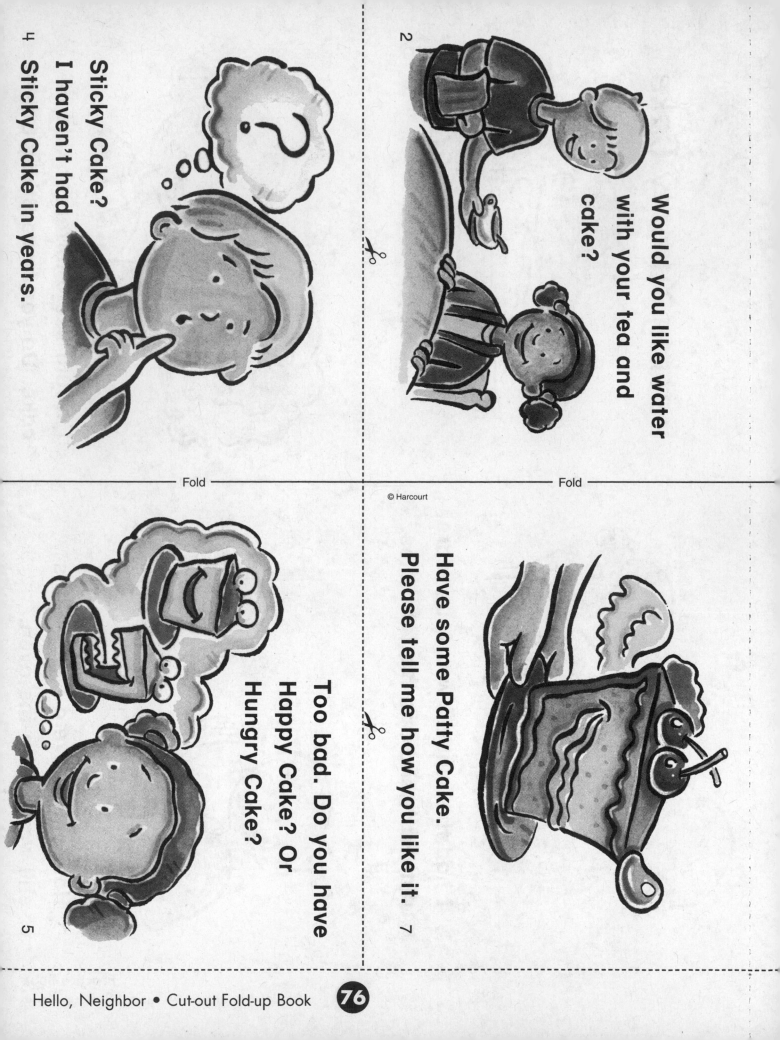

Would you like water
with your tea and
cake?

2

Fold

Sticky Cake?
I haven't had
Sticky Cake in years.

4

Fold

Have some Patty Cake.
Please tell me how you like it. 7

Too bad. Do you have
Happy Cake? Or
Hungry Cake?

5

© Harcourt

Hello, Neighbor • Cut-out Fold-up Book

76

One More Time

One likes to cook dinner.

Fold

Fold

© Harcourt

Four white birds smile and think
8 of their friend and his fine tales.

One bird wants to fly for miles and miles.

Five white birds share the same nest. They are together most of the time.

One bird tells tales from when he was young.

4

Why will this bird fly away? He'll go because he wants to see it one more time.

7

The others sit in front of him and listen. They smile and hide their beaks.

5

1

How to Make a Face

Fold

3

Always start with a nice, big circle.

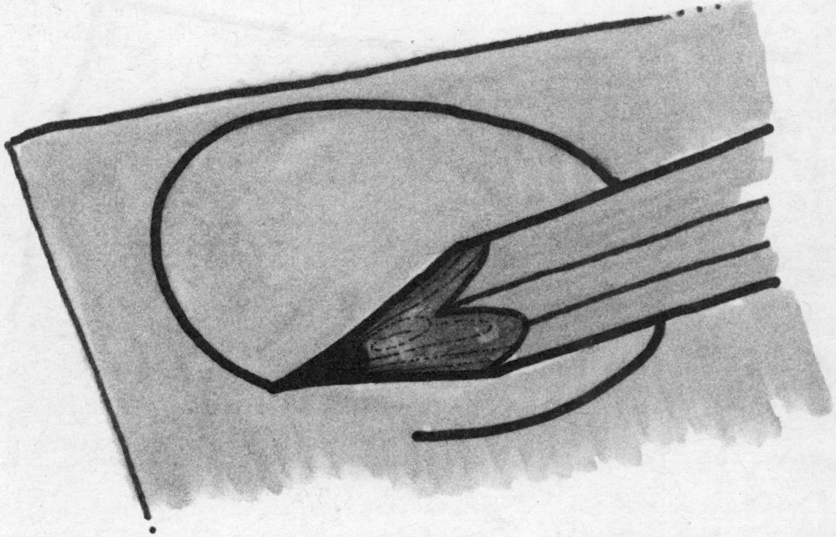

Fold

8

Now you make a face.

You're almost finished. Does it look pretty? You can make it fancy or simple.

6

Practice Book
Hello, Neighbor • Cut-out Fold-up Book

79

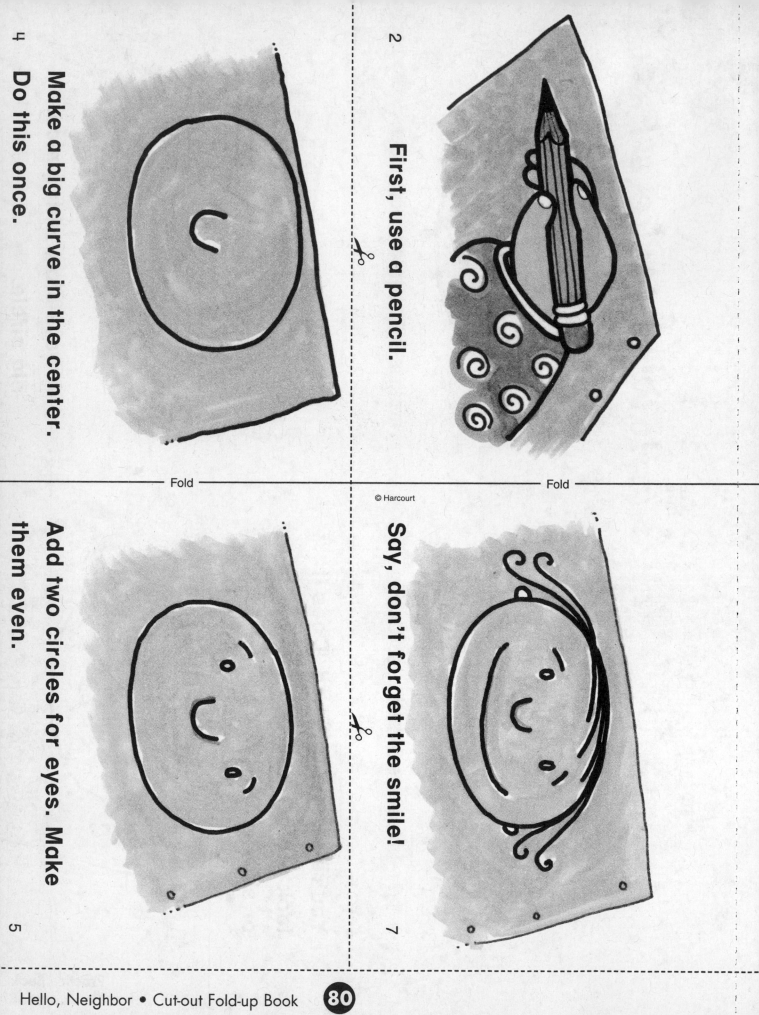

2 First, use a pencil.

4 Make a big curve in the center. Do this once.

7 Say, don't forget the smile!

5 Add two circles for eyes. Make them even.

Fold

Fold

© Harcourt

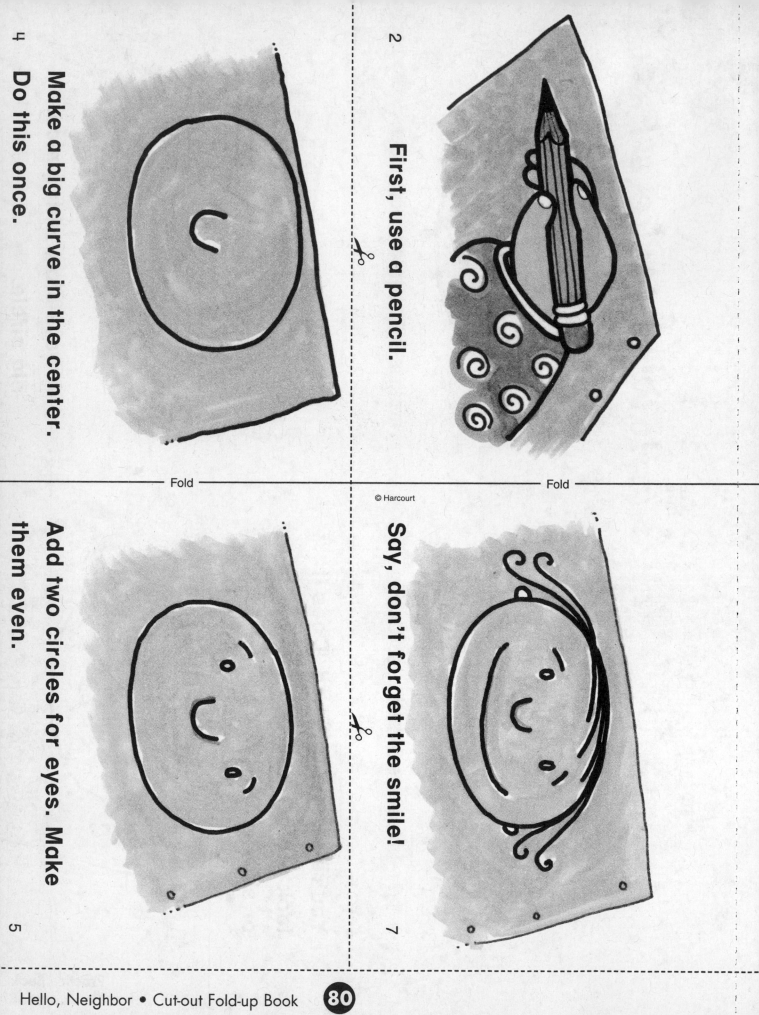

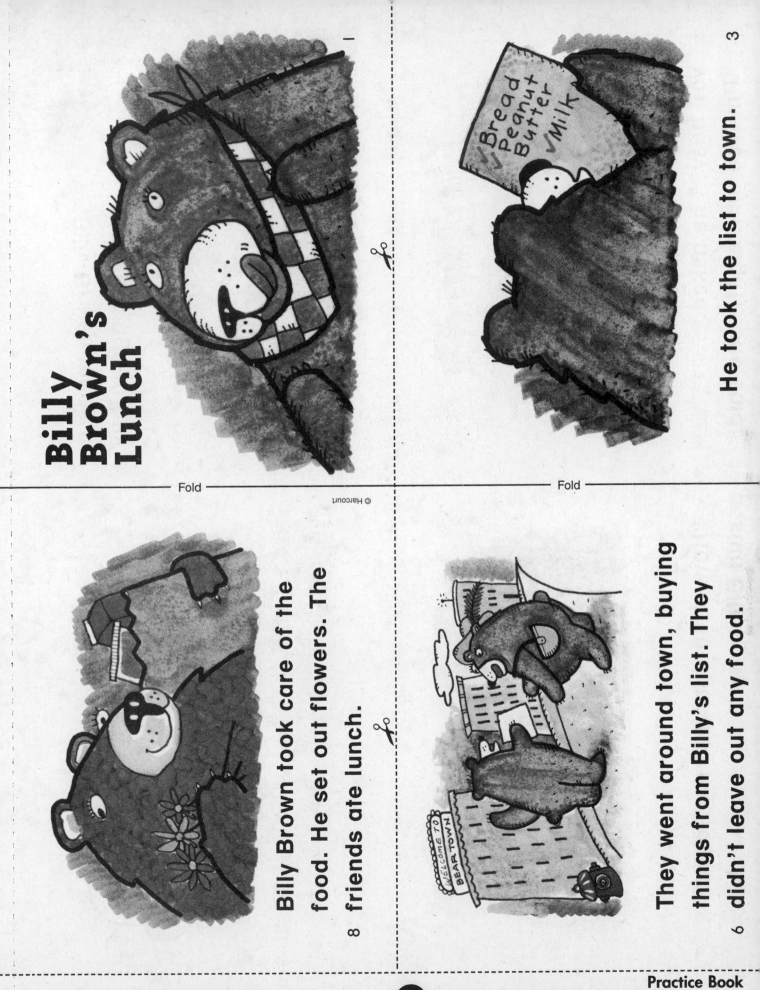

1

Billy Brown's Lunch

— Fold —

© Harcourt

3

He took the list to town.

— Fold —

Billy Brown took care of the food. He set out flowers. The friends ate lunch.

8

They went around town, buying things from Billy's list. They didn't leave out any food.

6

Billy Brown made a
list of things to buy.

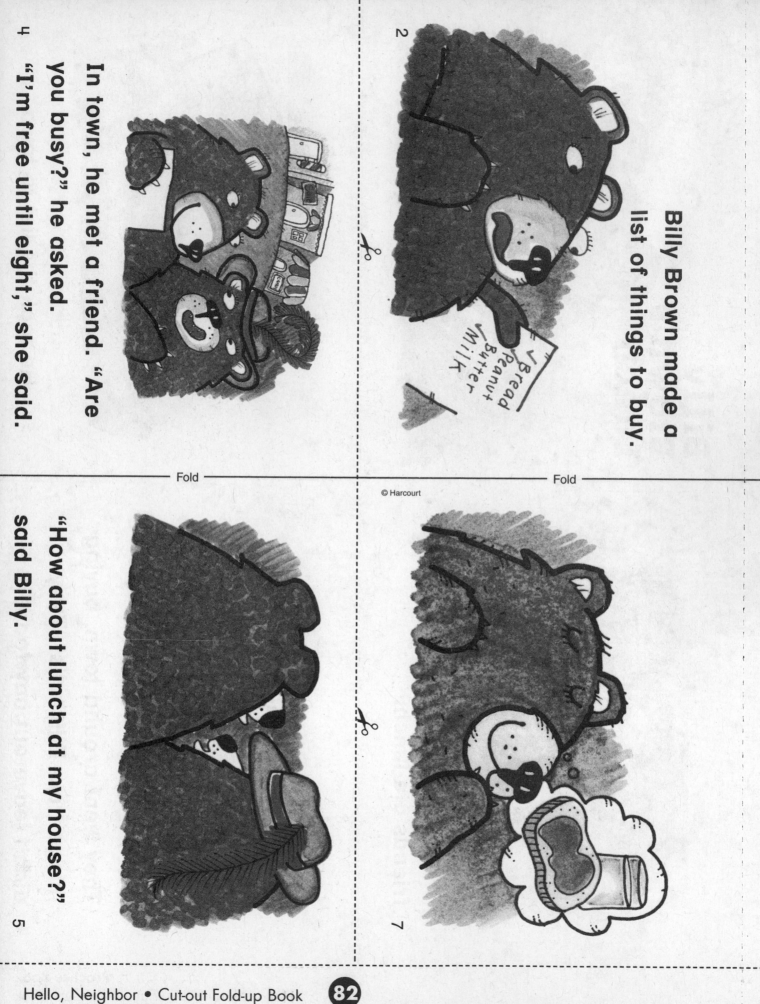

✓ Bread
✓ Peanut
✓ Butter
✓ Milk

Fold

4

In town, he met a friend. "Are
you busy?" he asked.
"I'm free until eight," she said.

Fold

"How about lunch at my house?"
said Billy.

5

7

A Dream to Fly

1

3

"Some day I'll go up in the sky. I want to try."

Fold

Fold

© Harcourt

Up in the sky, you will see

8 Mike fly, again and again.

Well, Mike got his wish.
He got in a plane.

6

Mike had a dream.
He wanted to fly.

4

Mike went to school. He wasn't
shy. He opened the doors.

Fold

Fold

"Hello from up here!
It's as easy as pie!"

7

"I'm going to fly. It's my dream
to be up in the sky."

5

Squirrels at Home

1

In fields and trees, wild squirrels scurry about.

3

Those squirrels are busy twelve months a year!

8

Squirrels quickly run up trees and poles. They can leap from branch to branch.

6

© Harcourt

At the change of
seasons, squirrels
dig holes to store
food. They are
busy as they
wait for winter.

Squirrels are found
all over the world.

---Fold---

© Harcourt

One squirrel doesn't want
another to touch its food.

---Fold---

Hello, Neighbor • Cut-out Fold-up Book

86

• T R O P H I E S •

Level Five

Gather Around

Name _____

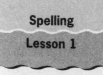

► **Read the words. Then read the name of each group. Write each word in the group where it belongs.**

Words That End With igh

_____

- - - - - - - - - - - -

_____

Words Without i

_____

- - - - - - - - - - - -

_____

- - - - - - - - - - - -

_____

_____

- - - - - - - - - - - -

_____

Words That End With ight

_____

- - - - - - - - - - - -

_____

- - - - - - - - - - - -

_____

_____

- - - - - - - - - - - -

_____

Spelling Words

high

night

light

right

might

bright

rode

those

touch

twelve

© Harcourt

SCHOOL-HOME CONNECTION Ask your child to read the Spelling Words aloud to you. Together, make up a little poem using some of the rhyming Spelling Words.

2

▶ **Circle the pictures whose names have the /ī/ sound. Then write the names of the pictures you circled.**

| high | fright | night | sigh | light |

1.

_____

- - - - - - -

_____

2.

_____

- - - - - - -

_____

3.

_____

- - - - - - -

_____

4.

_____

- - - - - - -

_____

5.

_____

- - - - - - -

_____

6.

_____

- - - - - - -

_____

© Harcourt

SCHOOL-HOME CONNECTION Ask your child to show you the completed page. Let your child explain why he or she did not write words for some exercises.

3

Practice Book
Gather Around • Lesson 1

Name _____

► **Add _er_ or _est_ to the word so that it correctly completes the sentence. Then write the word.**

bright

_____

- -

1. This bird has _____

colors than that bird.

_____

high

_____

- -

2. The blue bird lands on a _____

branch than the green bird.

_____

tight

_____

- -

3. Birds make nests in the _____

places.

TRY THIS With a partner, act out the words <u>light</u>, <u>lighter</u>, <u>lightest</u> and <u>high</u>, <u>higher</u>, <u>highest</u>.

© Harcourt

 SCHOOL-HOME CONNECTION Have your child read you the completed page, and show you how he or she chose how to answer.

 4

Name _____

▶ **The letters igh stand for the /ī/ sound.**
Circle the words that have the /ī/ sound.

1. branch	**2.** light
3. night	**4.** high
5. fright	**6.** nest

TRY THIS Write another word that rhymes with <u>sight</u>. Draw a picture for it. Then write a sentence using the word.

 SCHOOL-HOME CONNECTION Ask your child to show you the completed page. Let your child explain why he or she did *not* pick certain words.

 5

Practice Book
Gather Around • Lesson 1

© Harcourt

Name _____

► **Read the words in the box. Write the word that best completes each sentence.**

afraid	flew	learn	nothing	thought	wonder

1. Bob _____ off to join his friends.

2. He will _____ a lot out there.

3. I _____ where he is now.

4. I _____ he would be back by now.

5. Don't be _____. Bob will come back.

SCHOOL-HOME CONNECTION Ask your child to read aloud the sentences he or she completed. Then encourage your child to make up original sentences using the words in the box.

6

Practice Book
Gather Around • Lesson 1

© Harcourt

Name _____

▶ **Write the word from the box that names each picture.**

| feet | light | coat | night | seal | sigh |

1.

2.

3.

4.

5.

ahhh!

6.

SCHOOL-HOME CONNECTION Ask your child to read aloud the words he or she wrote to name the pictures. Together, think of words that rhyme with each of the words your child wrote.

Practice Book
Gather Around • Lesson 1

© Harcourt

Name _____

▶ **Read the story. Then read each pair of sentences. Circle the sentence that tells what happened in the story.**

"Where is my kitten? Have you seen my kitten?" asked Kip.

"No," said Mom. "Go and look."

So Kip went out to look for his kitten. He looked up in the tree. He looked under the bush and by the rocks. He saw some birds and bugs. He did not see his kitten.

Kip felt sad. He walked back to his door. There was his kitten, sitting on the mat!

1. Kip went out to look at the birds.
   Kip went out to look for his kitten.

2. Kip looked under the bush.
   Kip looked up in the sky.

3. Kip opened the door.
   Kip was sad until he saw his kitten.

 SCHOOL-HOME CONNECTION Ask your child to tell you about the story on this page. Then have your child read the story aloud to you.

8

Practice Book
Gather Around • Lesson 1

© Harcourt

Name _____

► **Read the word above each line. Add ed or ing to the word to complete the sentence. Remember to drop the final e.**

like

_____

- - - - - - - - - - - - - - - -

1. I have always _____ spring.

rake

_____

- - - - - - - - - - - - - - - -

2. My dad is _____ the fall leaves.

chase

_____

- - - - - - - - - - - - - - - -

3. I do not like _____ snowflakes.

make

_____

- - - - - - - - - - - - - - - -

4. Are you _____ a snowman?

bake

_____

- - - - - - - - - - - - - - - -

5. We _____ a cake.

SCHOOL-HOME CONNECTION Read the completed page with your child. Discuss your favorite seasons. Use words with -ed and -ing.

9

Practice Book
Gather Around • Lesson 1

© Harcourt

▶ **Read the words. Then read the name of each group. Write each word in the group where it belongs.**

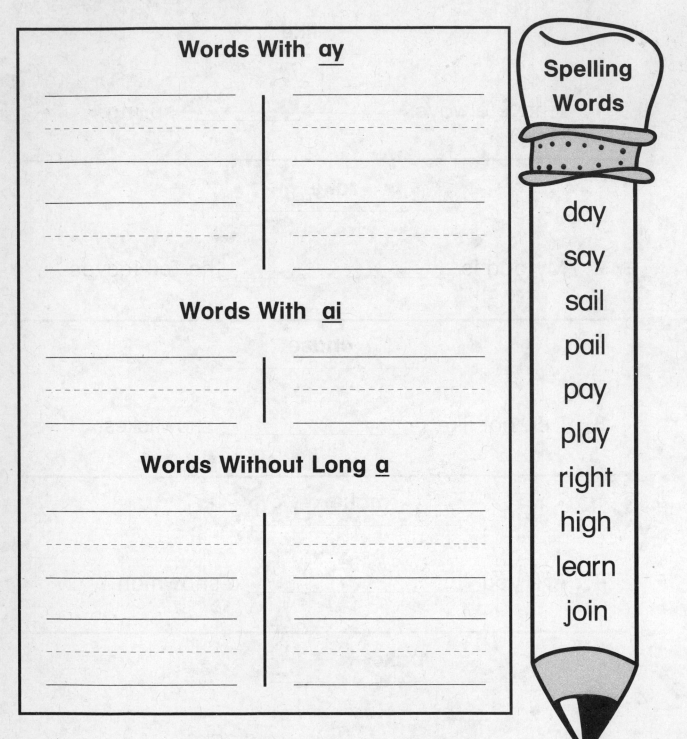

Words With <u>ay</u>

_____   _____

_____   _____

_____   _____

Words With <u>ai</u>

_____   _____

_____   _____

Words Without Long <u>a</u>

_____   _____

_____   _____

_____   _____

Spelling Words

day
say
sail
pail
pay
play
right
high
learn
join

© Harcourt

SCHOOL-HOME CONNECTION Have your child read the Spelling Words aloud to you. Ask your child which Spelling Words rhyme with *day*. Together, think of more words that rhyme with *day*.

10

Name _____

▶ **Circle the word that names the picture.**
Then write the word.

1.

hat   hot   hay

_____

- - - - - - - - - - - - - - - - -

_____

2.

pan   play   paint

_____

- - - - - - - - - - - - - - - - -

_____

3.

rain   ride   rail

_____

- - - - - - - - - - - - - - - - -

_____

4.

snack   sail   snail

_____

- - - - - - - - - - - - - - - - -

_____

5.

tray   tail   trap

_____

- - - - - - - - - - - - - - - - -

_____

6.

tree   tired   train

_____

- - - - - - - - - - - - - - - - -

_____

© Harcourt

TRY THIS Write a word that rhymes with <u>hay</u> and has <u>ay</u>. Write a word that rhymes with <u>snail</u> and has <u>ai</u>. Draw a picture for each word.

 SCHOOL-HOME CONNECTION Ask your child to share the finished page with you. Together, make up a sentence for each answer.

 11

Practice Book
Gather Around • Lesson 2

Name _____

► **Look at the picture. Write a verb to complete each sentence.**

play	stay	wait	mail

_____

1. Frog wanted Toad to _____ ball.

_____

2. Toad wanted to _____ a letter first.

_____

3. Frog said, "I will sit and _____ for you."

_____

4. Toad asked Frog to _____ for supper.

 TRY THIS Work with a partner. Make a list of as many verbs as you can.

SCHOOL-HOME CONNECTION With your child, look for some other verbs on this page. (asked, said, wanted)

Practice Book
Gather Around • Lesson 2

© Harcourt

Name _____

▶ **Write the word from the box that best completes each sentence.**

| play | stay | day | rain | wait |

_____

1. I do not like the _____.

_____

2. I can't _____ outside.

_____

3. I don't want to _____ home.

_____

4. I want a sunny _____.

_____

5. I will _____

for the sun to come out.

TRY THIS Use the words <u>mail</u>, <u>day</u>, and <u>gray</u> to write a short poem or story about the weather.

SCHOOL-HOME CONNECTION Ask your child to read you the completed page. Together, make up a few sentences about what the toad did after the sun came out. Use words with *ai* and *ay*.

▲13

© Harcourt

Name _____

▶ **Read the words in the box. Write the word that best completes each sentence.**

caught	cold	hurried	near	son	sure

1. Mr. Bates took his _____ fishing.

2. They went to a lake _____ their house.

3. The day was _____ and wet, but they had fun.

5. "Look at what I _____," said his son.

6. They _____ home with the big fish.

SCHOOL-HOME CONNECTION Ask your child to read aloud the sentences he or she completed. Together, talk about some of the things sons and daughters like to do with other family members.

14

Practice Book
Gather Around • Lesson 2

© Harcourt

▶ **Write the words where they belong in the puzzle.**

| gate | lake | nail | rain | hay | rake |

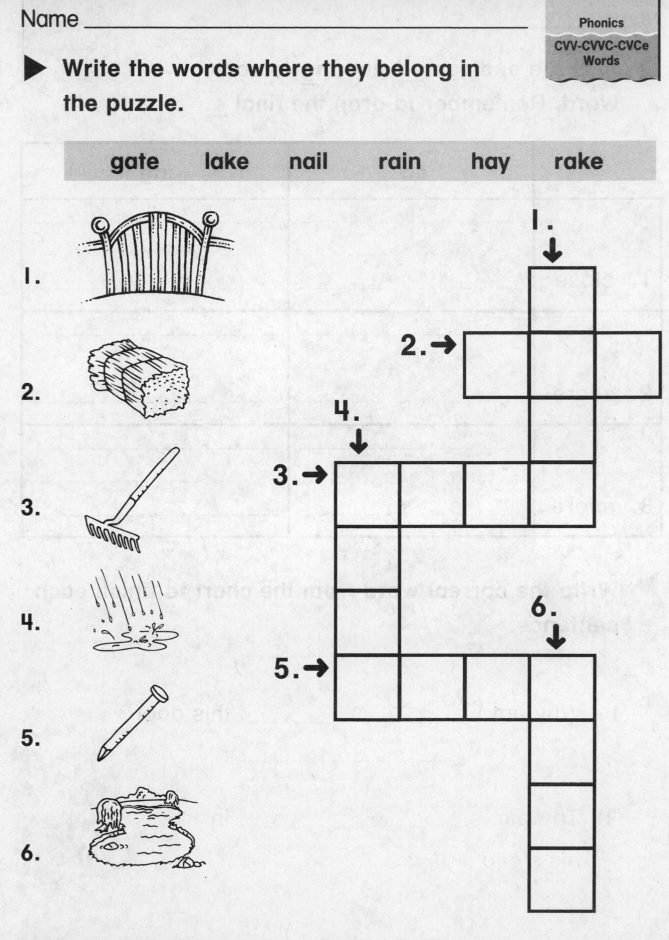

1.

2.

3.

4.

5.

6.

SCHOOL-HOME CONNECTION Have your child name each picture and point to the word in the puzzle. Together, think of words that rhyme with some of the words.

15

Practice Book
Gather Around • Lesson 2

Name _____

► **Add the endings <u>ed</u> and <u>ing</u> to each word. Remember to drop the final <u>e</u>.**

	ed	ing
1. close		
2. scare		
3. snore		

► **Write the correct word from the chart to finish each sentence.**

1. Why am I _____ this door?

2. The pig is _____ in his sleep.

SCHOOL-HOME CONNECTION Read your
child's completed sentences aloud. Have him
or her say "stop" when you get to a word with
an *-ing* ending.

16

Practice Book
Gather Around • Lesson 2

© Harcourt

▶ **Read the words. Then read the name of each group. Write each word in the group where it belongs.**

Words With ind	**Words With ild**
_____	_____
- - - - - - - - -	- - - - - - - - -
_____	_____
_____	_____
_____	_____
_____	_____

Words Without i

_____	_____
- - - - - - - - -	- - - - - - - - -
_____	_____
- - - - - - - - -	- - - - - - - - -
_____	_____

Spelling Words

find
kind
mind
mild
child
wild
day
play
sure
son

SCHOOL-HOME CONNECTION Ask your child to read the Spelling Words aloud to you. Take turns making up sentences using two or three of the Spelling Words.

© Harcourt

Name _____

▶ **Choose a word in the box that rhymes with each underlined word and makes sense. Write it on the line.**

find	behind	wild

1. Do you <u>mind</u>? There's a big

_____

frog _____ us.

2. At the zoo, a <u>child</u> saw these words:

_____

"Do not feed our _____

animals."

3. You need to <u>wind</u> this toy.

_____

The baby will _____

it and play with it.

TRY THIS Make your own pair of sentences with two words from the box or other words that rhyme with them.

SCHOOL-HOME CONNECTION Discuss the finished page with your child. Help him or her notice the long *i* sound in each word

18

© Harcourt

Name _____

▶ **Write the verb that best completes each sentence.**

drink	find	help	make	fill

1. I _____ the bird bath.

2. Birds _____ from it.

3. They come and _____ seeds in our feeder.

4. We _____ birds because we like them.

5. I _____ bird feeders for my friends, too.

TRY THIS Work with a friend to read a news story about a sports team. Together, find the verbs that tell about now.

SCHOOL-HOME CONNECTION Have your child read you the completed page. Together, make up more sentences that use the verbs from this page.

Practice Book
Gather Around • Lesson 3

© Harcourt

► **Write the word from the box that best completes each sentence.**

find	behind	wild	blind	mind

1. It can see.

_____

It is not _____.

2. It is not tame.

_____

It is _____.

3. It is not lost.

_____

I can _____ it.

4. A tadpole's tail is not in front.

_____

It is _____.

5. A tadpole doesn't think like we do.

_____

It has a _____ of its own.

SCHOOL-HOME CONNECTION Ask your child to show you the finished page. Together use the sentences to make up a definition for each word in the box.

20

© Harcourt

Name _____

▶ **Circle the word that best completes each sentence. Then write the word.**

both
during
ready

1. Are _____ bears sleeping?

---

both
during
ready

2. Yes, they sleep _____ the winter.

---

both
during
ready

3. In spring they are _____ to wake up.

---

both
during
ready

4. Then they will _____ catch fish.

---

both
during
ready

5. They will be _____ to eat.

SCHOOL–HOME CONNECTION Ask your child to read aloud the sentences he or she completed. Together, make up other sentences using the words *both*, *during*, and *ready*.

21

Practice Book
Gather Around • Lesson 3

© Harcourt

Name _____

▶ **Write the word from the box that best completes each sentence.**

hide	child	kite	like	wild

_____

1. Who is that _____?

_____

_____

2. She will _____ by that big tree.

_____

_____

3. She has a great _____.

_____

_____

4. The wind is _____ today.

_____

_____

5. We all _____ kites.

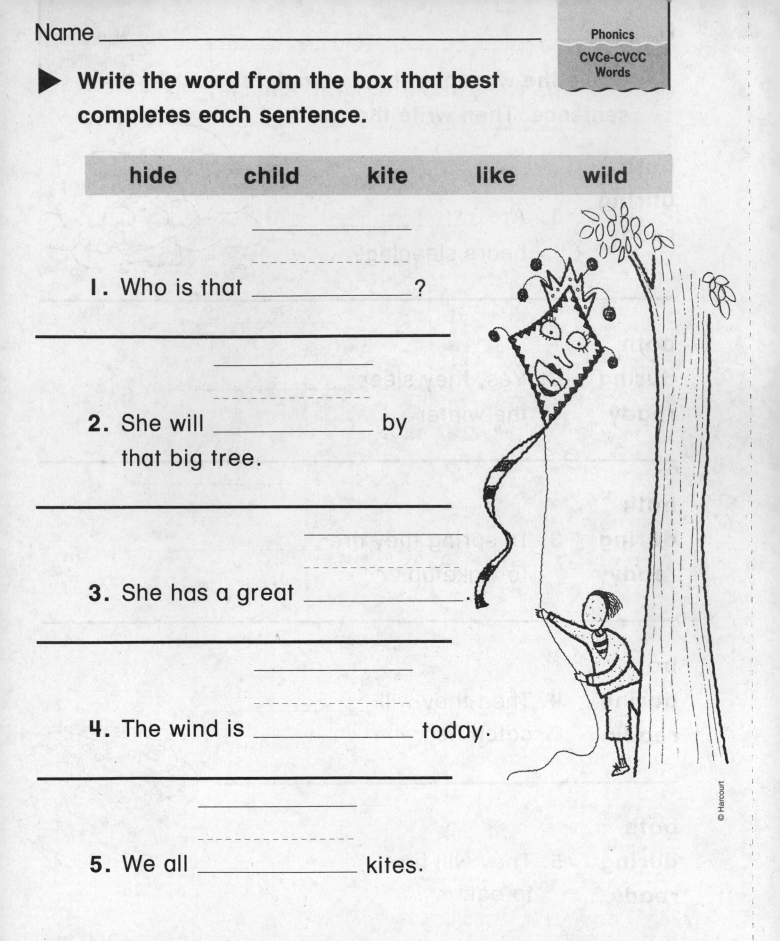

 SCHOOL-HOME CONNECTION Have your child read aloud the sentences he or she completed. Then take turns saying sentences about things you like.

 22

Practice Book
Gather Around • Lesson 3

© Harcourt

Name _____

▶ **Read the paragraph. Write the main idea in the box. Write the details in the circles.**

Ducks are born knowing many things. Ducklings know that they must follow their mother. Ducklings also know how to swim. The mother does not have to show them.

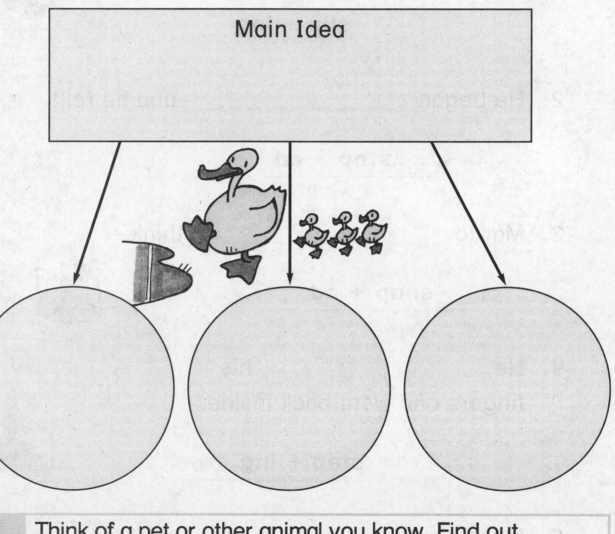

Main Idea

 TRY THIS Think of a pet or other animal you know. Find out what things that animal knows when it is born. Find out what things the animal has to learn.

 SCHOOL-HOME CONNECTION Ask your child to read the paragraph at the top of this page to you. Together, think of a title for the paragraph.

 23

Practice Book
Gather Around • Lesson 3

© Harcourt

Name _____

▶ **Look at the words and endings. Write the word that completes the sentence. Double the last letter before you add _ed_ or _ing_.**

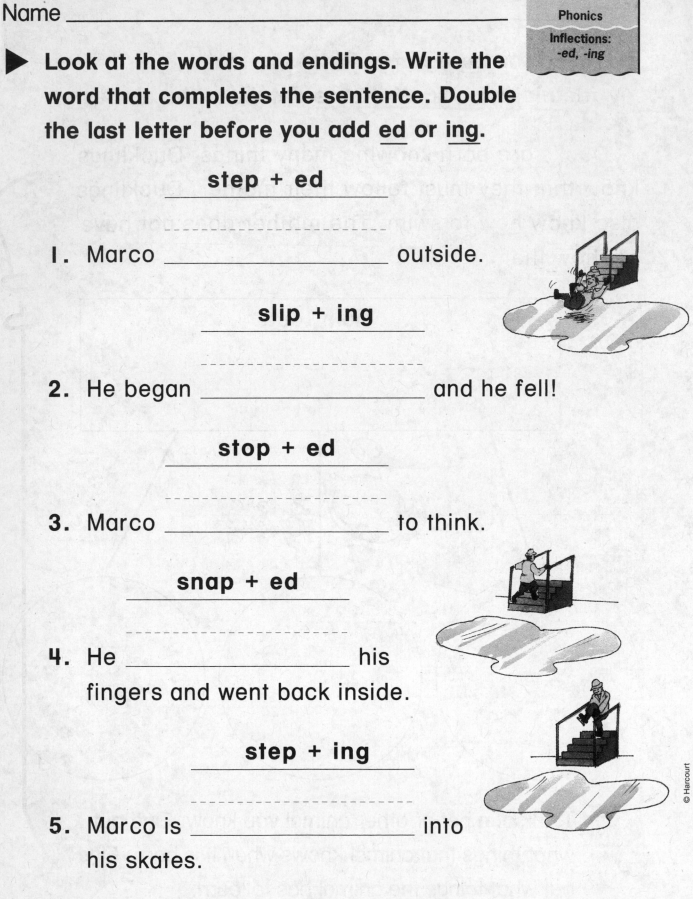

step + ed
_____

1. Marco _____ outside.

slip + ing
_____

2. He began _____ and he fell!

stop + ed
_____

3. Marco _____ to think.

snap + ed
_____

4. He _____ his fingers and went back inside.

step + ing
_____

5. Marco is _____ into his skates.

 SCHOOL-HOME CONNECTION Ask your child to read you the completed page. Work together to write new sentences for the answer words.

24

Practice Book
Gather Around • Lesson 3

© Harcourt

Name _____

► **Read the words. Then read the name of each group. Write each word in the group where it belongs.**

Words With <u>old</u>	**Other Words With <u>o</u>**
_____	_____
_____	_____
_____	_____
_____	_____
_____	_____
_____	_____

Words Without <u>o</u>

_____	_____
_____	_____

Spelling Words

old

fold

told

cold

roll

most

find

child

both

during

SCHOOL-HOME CONNECTION Ask your child to read the Spelling Words aloud. Take turns making up sentences with two or three of the words.

25

© Harcourt

Name _____

▶ **Read the numbered clues. Use the words from the box to complete the puzzle.**

hello	gold	no	also
ago	cold	soda	go

Across

2. a long time ___

3. ____ pop

4. stop and __

6. _____, how are you?

Down

1. icy ____

2. me ____ (too)

4. silver and ____

5. __, thanks

© Harcourt

SCHOOL-HOME CONNECTION Ask your child to share the completed page. Then work together to list some words that rhyme with *old* and to write some clues for these words. See if a friend can guess the words.

26

▶ **Write <u>am</u>, <u>is</u>, or <u>are</u> to finish each sentence.**

_____
- - - - - - - -

1. What _____ you doing?

_____
- - - - - - - -

2. I _____ playing with a yo-yo.

_____
- - - - - - - -

3. _____ you good at it?

_____
- - - - - - - -

4. My sister _____ better.

_____
- - - - - - - -

5. She _____ standing over there.

_____
- - - - - - - -

6. I _____ taking lessons from her.

TRY THIS Work with a partner to answer the question "What are you doing?" Answer two ways—beginning with "I am" and with "We are."

© Harcourt

► **Choose the word that best completes each sentence. Then write the word.**

fold   old   told

_____

- - - - - - - - - - - - -

I. Mr. Rabbit broke his _____ bed.

go   so   got

_____

- - - - - - - - - - - - -

2. Mr. and Mrs. Rabbit _____ get a new bed.

soda   spot   sofa

_____

- - - - - - - - - - - - -

3. Mr. Rabbit sees a nice _____ bed.

Old   Sold   Socks

_____

- - - - - - - - - - - - -

4. Mr. and Mrs. Rabbit say, "_____!"

TRY THIS Make up rhyming sentences using the words <u>sold</u>, <u>old</u>, and <u>told</u>. Say your sentences to classmates.

SCHOOL-HOME CONNECTION Have your child find the long *o* words that were not used as answers. Ask him or her to read them aloud and explain why they weren't the answers.

28

© Harcourt

Name _____

▶ **Read the words in the box. Write the word that best completes each sentence.**

clues	detective	floor	nature	piece	pulls

_____

1. I like to watch what happens in _____.

_____

2. The bird _____ up a bit of yarn.

_____

3. Now it has a little _____ of cloth.

_____

4. These are _____ to what the bird
   is doing.

_____

5. It is making the _____ of
   its nest soft.

SCHOOL-HOME CONNECTION Have your child read aloud the sentences he or she completed. Then take turns making up other sentences using the words in the box.

29

© Harcourt

Name _____

▶ **Circle the sentence that tells about each picture.**

1. "Let's go!" said the colt.

   "No!" said the girl.

   "Hello!" said the ant.

2. A pig thinks he is cold.

   A pig thinks he has lost his gold.

   A pig thinks he has lost his bone.

3. I am going home now.

   I am over on the sofa.

   I am holding the gold in this safe.

4. I have a total of 3 bags.

   I have a total of 3 ropes.

   I have a total of 3 bones.

5. "Have no fear! Cold soda is here!"

   "Have no fear! Your roses are here!"

   "Have no fear! Colt and the gold are here!"

6. The pig holds his gold.

   The colt keeps the gold.

   The colt calls the pig.

© Harcourt

SCHOOL-HOME CONNECTION Review the completed page with your child. Then make up a new adventure for the superhero colt.

30

Practice Book
Gather Around • Lesson 4

Name _____

► **Read the selection. Find the sentence that tells the main idea. Write it on the lines. Then write a title for the selection.**

Title

_____

- - - - - - - - - - - - - - - - - - - -

_____

Much more than water is in the sea. The sea is filled with living things. Many animals and plants live there. Some of the animals look like plants. We use many of the living things that are in the sea.

Main Idea

_____

- - - - - - - - - - - - - - - - - - - -

_____

- - - - - - - - - - - - - - - - - - - -

_____

- - - - - - - - - - - - - - - - - - - -

_____

 SCHOOL-HOME CONNECTION Read a picture book with your child. Discuss the main idea of the story.

 31

Practice Book
Gather Around • Lesson 4

Name _____

▶ **Finish each sentence. Write the contraction for the two words above it.**

| They've | You've | You'd | We'd | We're |

We are

_____

- - - - - - - - - - - - - -

1. _____ in our new bed.

We would

_____

- - - - - - - - - - - - - -

2. _____ love you to come see.

You have

_____

- - - - - - - - - - - - - -

3. _____ been here before.

They have

_____

- - - - - - - - - - - - - -

4. _____ got their own bed.

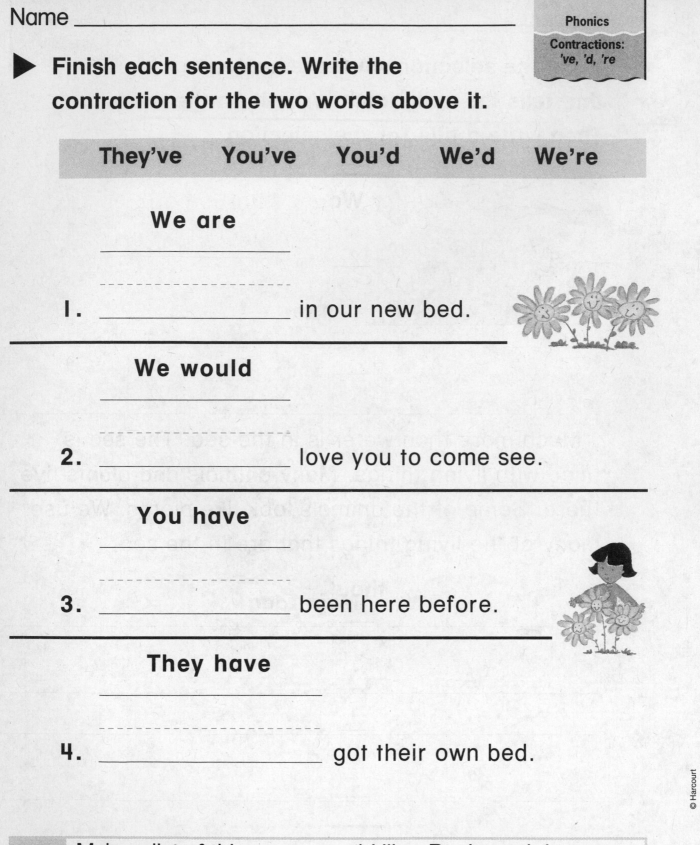

TRY THIS Make a list of things you would like. Begin each item on your list with the words I'd like.

 SCHOOL-HOME CONNECTION Ask your child to read the completed page aloud to you. Help your child use each contraction in a sentence.

 32

Practice Book
Gather Around • Lesson 4

© Harcourt

Name _____

▶ **Read the words. Then read the name of each group. Write each word in the group where it belongs.**

Words That End With <u>age</u>

_____

- - - - - - - - - - - - - - - - -

_____

- - - - - - - - - - - - - - - - -

_____

_____

Words That End With <u>dge</u>

_____

- - - - - - - - - - - - - - - - -

_____

- - - - - - - - - - - - - - - - -

_____

_____

Words Without <u>g</u>

_____

- - - - - - - - - - - - - - - - -

_____

_____

_____

- - - - - - - - - - - - - - - - -

_____

_____

Spelling Words

age
page
cage
badge
budge
fudge
old
most
floor
piece

SCHOOL-HOME CONNECTION With your child, read the Spelling Words out loud. Together, try to make up a sentence using five—or even more—of the words.

33

Practice Book
Gather Around • Lesson 5

© Harcourt

Name _____

▶ **Write the word from the box that best completes each sentence.**

| large | age | bridge | edge |

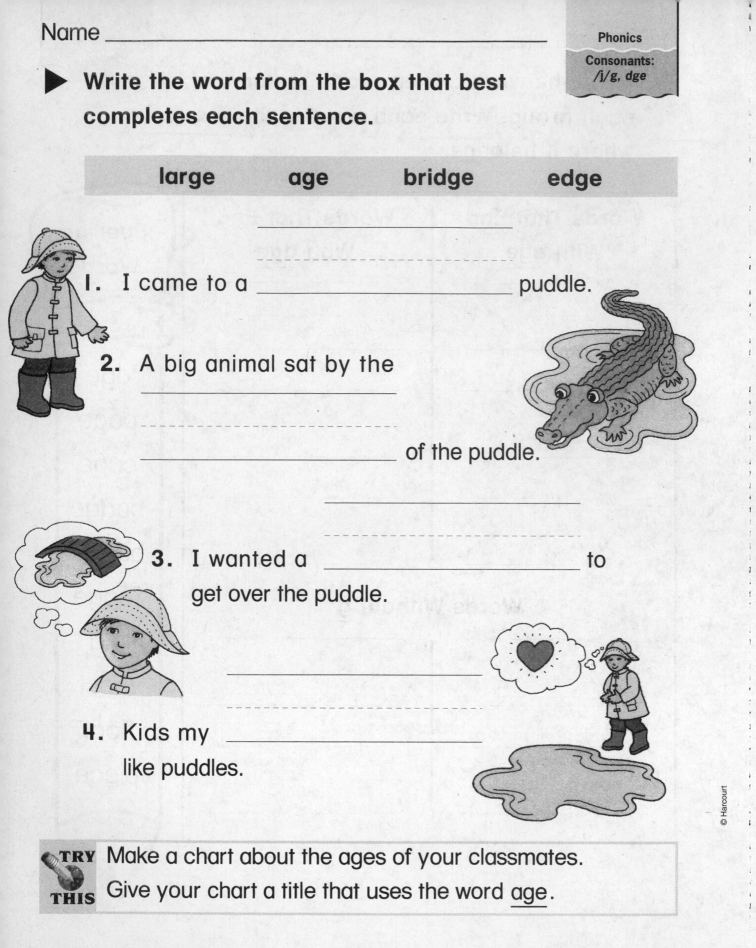

_____

1. I came to a _____ puddle.

2. A big animal sat by the

_____

_____ of the puddle.

_____

3. I wanted a _____ to
   get over the puddle.

_____

4. Kids my _____
   like puddles.

TRY THIS Make a chart about the ages of your classmates.
Give your chart a title that uses the word <u>age</u>.

SCHOOL-HOME CONNECTION Ask your child
to read you the finished page. Together, think
of as many words as you can that have the soft
g sound.

34

© Harcourt

Name _____

▶ **Write the word that best completes each sentence.**

| spilled | filled | needed | cleaned |

_____
- -

1. Lenny _____ to make some ice.

_____
- - - - - - - - - - - - - - - - -

2. He _____ the ice tray with water.

_____
- - - - - - - - - - - - - - - - - - -

3. The water _____ all over.

_____
- - - - - - - - - - - - - - - - -

4. Lenny _____ up

the mess.

TRY THIS With a partner, take turns reading the sentences and acting them out.

SCHOOL-HOME CONNECTION Have your child read the completed page to you. Ask him or her to tell you what the action words would be if they were about the present time.

▲35▲

Practice Book
Gather Around • Lesson 5

© Harcourt

Name _____

▶ **Look at the picture. Then do what the sentences tell you to do.**

1. Make the pig on stage pink.

2. Give the pig a huge hat.

3. Find the largest bed. Put a badge on it.

4. Draw a huge pillow on one edge of a bed.

5. Find the cage next to the largest bed. Draw a pet gerbil inside the cage.

6. A large crowd is watching from the bridge. Draw a ring around the large crowd.

TRY THIS Write a sentence about this picture. Use some of the words from the sentences on the page.

 SCHOOL-HOME CONNECTION Go over the completed page with your child. Then have your child circle the words that contain the /j/ sound spelled with *g*.

© Harcourt

▶ **Write the word from the box that best completes each sentence.**

| angry | nearly | okay | sorry |

1.

I hope you are

_____

- - - - - - - - - - - - - - - - - -

_____ .

2.

_____

- - - - - - - - - - - - - - - - - -

I _____

fell down.

3.

_____

- - - - - - - - - - - - - - - - - -

I'm _____

I bumped into you.

4.

I hope you are not

_____

- - - - - - - - - - - - - - - - - -

_____ !

SCHOOL-HOME CONNECTION Ask your child to read aloud the sentences he or she completed. Then take turns making up your own sentences using the words in the box.

37

Practice Book
Gather Around • Lesson 5

© Harcourt

Name _____

▶ **Circle the word that names each picture.**
Then write the word.

I.

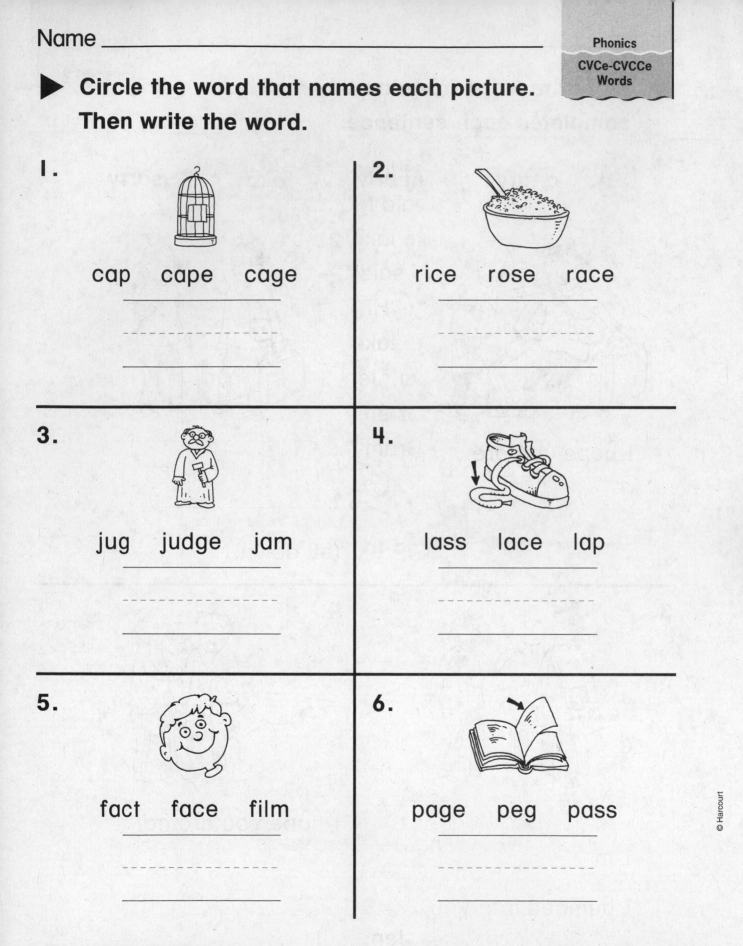

cap   cape   cage

_____

- - - - - - - - - -

2.

rice   rose   race

_____

- - - - - - - - - -

3.

jug   judge   jam

_____

- - - - - - - - - -

4.

lass   lace   lap

_____

- - - - - - - - - -

5.

fact   face   film

_____

- - - - - - - - - -

6.

page   peg   pass

_____

- - - - - - - - - -

SCHOOL-HOME CONNECTION Have your
child read aloud the words he or she wrote on
this page. Then point to some of the other
words under the pictures, and ask your child to
read them, too.

38

© Harcourt

Name _____

▶ **Read the story. Then complete the sentences.**

"Will you take me to the lake, Mom?" asked Jen.

"No. I have to work," said Mom.

"Will you take me to the lake, Dad?" asked Jen.

"No. I have lots to do," said Dad.

Just then, Gram called. "Hi, Gram," said Jen.

"Will you take me to the lake?"

"That's why I called you, Jen. I want to take you to the lake," said Gram.

"Oh good! Thank you Gram," said Jen.

_____

1. Jen wanted to go to _____.

2. _____ said no.

3. _____ said no, too.

4. _____ said she would take Jen.

SCHOOL-HOME CONNECTION Have your child read the story to you. Then ask how your child knew the answers to the questions.

39

Practice Book
Gather Around • Lesson 5

© Harcourt

Name _____

▶ **Write the contraction from the box for the two words above each sentence.**

| I'd | We're | We'd | You're | I've |

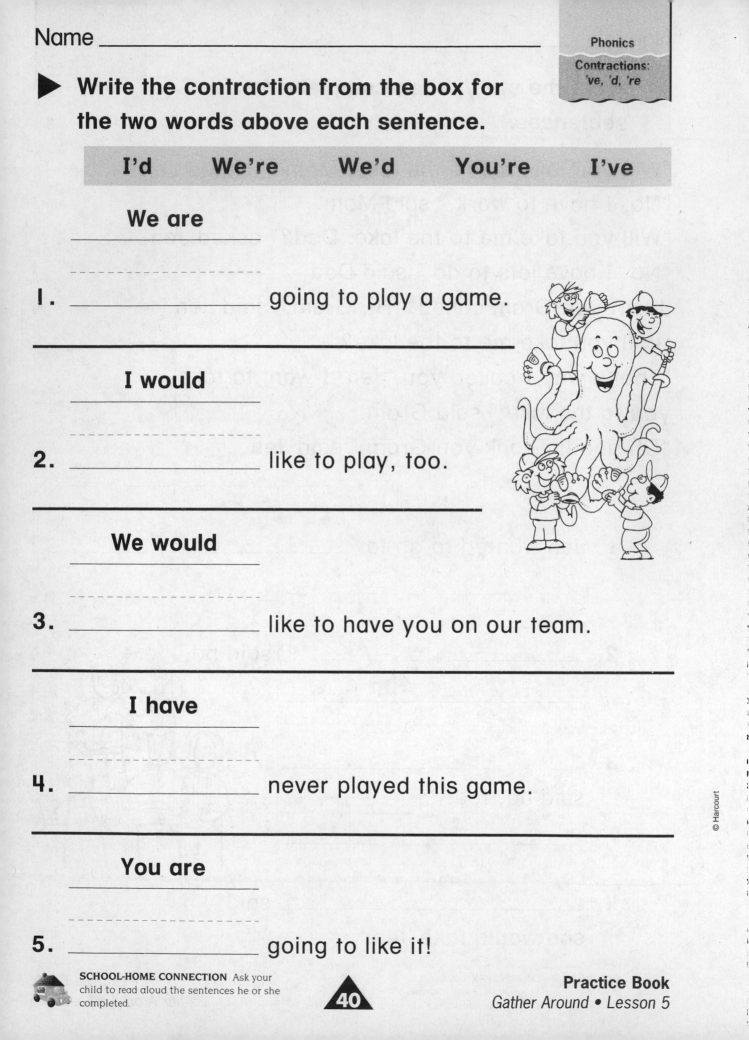

We are
_____

1. _____ going to play a game.

I would
_____

2. _____ like to play, too.

We would
_____

3. _____ like to have you on our team.

I have
_____

4. _____ never played this game.

You are
_____

5. _____ going to like it!

SCHOOL-HOME CONNECTION Ask your child to read aloud the sentences he or she completed.

40

Practice Book
Gather Around • Lesson 5

© Harcourt

► **Read the words. Then read the name of each group. Write each word in the group where it belongs.**

Words With Silent e

_____ _____

_____ _____

_____ _____

_____ _____

_____ _____

_____ _____

_____ _____

Words With y

_____ _____

Spelling Words

tube
cube
cute
use
rule
huge
page
fudge
angry
sorry

 SCHOOL-HOME CONNECTION Have your child read the Spelling Words aloud to you. Then ask your child which two Spelling Words rhyme.

 41

Name _____

► **Circle the word that best completes each sentence. Then write the word.**

1. The cat looked up and said, "It is

_____

- -

_____!"

hand
huge
tube

_____

- - - - - - - - - - - - - - - - - - - -

2. "It smells like _____," said the mule.

perfume
cute
perform

3. The cat sniffed but could not smell

_____

- - - - - - - - - - - - - - - - -

the _____.

purple
perfume
huge

_____

- - - - - - - - - - - - - - -

4. "_____ me, but it has no smell," said the cat.

Every
Excuse
Cube

_____

- - - - - - - - - - - - - - -

5. "Oh! _____ me!" said the mule. "I was sniffing a flower."

Empty
Plume
Excuse

SCHOOL-HOME CONNECTION Ask your child to read the completed page to you. Then ask your child to explain in his or her own words what the story is about.

42

© Harcourt

Name _____

▶ **Write was or were to complete each sentence. Then circle one or more than one to show how many people or things the action word tells about.**

1. I _____ skating all day.   one   more than one

2. They _____ skating, too.   one   more than one

3. We _____ in a pile!   one   more than one

4. We _____ all okay.   one   more than one

TRY THIS With a classmate, tell about three things that happened yesterday. Use was and were in your discussion.

SCHOOL-HOME CONNECTION Ask your child to read this page to you and explain his or her answers.

43

© Harcourt

Name _____

▶ **Write words from the box to complete the story.**

cube	huge	Use	cute

"I am never coming out," sniffled Mole. "I am small,

_____

but I want to be _____. I want my den to be

_____

shaped like a _____."

"_____ this," said Mule, as she gave a book

to Mole. "You are _____. You are my friend,"

Mole said, and she came out.

SCHOOL-HOME CONNECTION Work with
your child to write original sentences for the
words *cute, huge, cube,* and *use.*

44

Practice Book
Gather Around • Lesson 6

Name _____

► **Write the word that best completes
each sentence.**

boy	brought	few	head	read

1. This _____ won the contest!

2. He was standing on his _____
   for a long time.

3. He _____ a book
   at the same time.

4. He even ate a _____ crackers.

5. Who _____
   the boy his prize?

SCHOOL-HOME CONNECTION Ask your child
to read the completed sentences to you. Then
take turns making up your own sentences using
the words in the box.

45

Name _____

▶ **Write the word from the box that names each picture.**

| bike | cone | cube | gate | mule | tube |

1.

_____

- - - - - - - - - - - -

_____

2.

_____

- - - - - - - - - - - -

_____

3.

_____

- - - - - - - - - - - -

_____

4.

_____

- - - - - - - - - - - -

_____

5.

_____

- - - - - - - - - - - -

_____

6.

_____

- - - - - - - - - - - -

_____

 SCHOOL-HOME CONNECTION Ask your child to read aloud the words he or she wrote to name the pictures. Then take turns making up sentences using some of the words.

46

© Harcourt

Name _____

▶ **Choose the word that finishes each**
sentence. Write it on the line.

plan   planned   planning

_____

1. I had _____ to go to bed.

wagged   wag   wagging

_____

2. My dog was _____ his tail.

tapped   tap   tapping

_____

3. Who is _____ at the door?

hugging   hug   hugged

_____

4. I _____ my grandma at

the door.

SCHOOL-HOME CONNECTION Ask your child
to read the completed page to you. Together,
write sentences for some of the answer choices
not used.

47

Practice Book
Gather Around • Lesson 6

© Harcourt

► **Read the words. Then read the name of each group. Write each word in the group where it belongs.**

Words With ea

_____ _____
_____ _____
_____ _____
_____ _____
_____ _____
_____ _____

Words Without ea

_____ _____
_____ _____
_____ _____
_____ _____

Spelling Words

lead
head
bread
read
ready
heavy
rule
use
few
boy

© Harcourt

SCHOOL-HOME CONNECTION Ask your child to read the Spelling Words aloud to you. Then take turns making up sentences that begin with *I'm ready.*

48

Practice Book
Gather Around • Lesson 7

Name _____

▶ **Finish each sentence. Circle the word that makes sense and has the same vowel sound as the underlined word. Then write the word.**

feather
bread
meat

1. I <u>fed</u> the bird. I gave it some

_____

- -

_____ .

---

meal
breakfast
breath

2. I like to <u>help</u>. Today I made

_____

- -

_____ .

---

breakfast
heat
weather

3. I'll go with <u>them</u> even in bad

_____

- -

_____ .

---

instead
real
head

4. I sleep in my <u>bed</u>.
My bird rests on the sand

_____

- -

_____ .

SCHOOL-HOME CONNECTION Have your child explain how he or she chose the answers.

49

Name _____

▶ **Write <u>go</u> or <u>went</u> to complete each sentence. Then circle <u>now</u> or <u>in the past</u> to show when each action took place.**

1. You and I can _____ to the zoo.

    now
    in the past

2. We _____ last month.

    now
    in the past

3. We can _____ again.

    now
    in the past

4. The goats _____ from rock to rock last time.

    now
    in the past

TRY THIS Work with a partner to change each sentence. If it is in the past, make it tell about now. If it is about now, make it tell about something in the past. Use the words <u>go</u> and <u>went</u>.

© Harcourt

SCHOOL-HOME CONNECTION Share the completed page with your child. If he or she is confused about the term "in the past," use the word "before" instead.

50

Practice Book
Gather Around • Lesson 7

Name _____

▶ **Read the sentences. Do what they tell you. Circle the words that have the /e/ vowel sound.**

What Is Up Ahead?

1. It has feathers. Color the feathers blue.

2. Its web is spread between the branches. Color it red.

3. It is heavy and has a huge head. Color it gray.

4. It looks like bad weather. Color the storm clouds.

5. A big animal is taking a bath. Color it green.

 TRY THIS Make funny or scary warning signs. Each one should include the word <u>ahead</u>.

 SCHOOL-HOME CONNECTION Share the completed page with your child. Find the words with the short *e* sound spelled *ea*. Work together to make up new sentences for those words.

 51

Practice Book
Gather Around • Lesson 7

© Harcourt

Name _____

► **Write the word from the box that best completes each sentence.**

| afternoon | bicycle | carry | hours | parents |

_____

1. I have a new _____.

_____

2. We can _____

it on the back of our car.

_____

3. My _____ and I

like to ride together.

_____

4. We can ride for _____!

_____

5. I hope we can go riding this _____.

SCHOOL-HOME CONNECTION Have your
child read aloud the sentences he or she
completed. Then talk about what your child
likes to do in the afternoon..

52

© Harcourt

▶ **Circle the word that names the picture.**
Then write the word.

1.

third   thud   thread

_____

- - - - - - - - - - -

2.

bead   bad   bed

_____

- - - - - - - - - - -

3.

ten   ton   teen

_____

- - - - - - - - - - -

4.

had   head   help

_____

- - - - - - - - - - -

5.

bird   bread   broth

_____

- - - - - - - - - - -

6.

weep   when   web

_____

- - - - - - - - - - -

Name _____

▶ **Read the selection. Circle the main idea
and write four details. Write one detail on each rock.**

In 1997, people learned a lot about Mars from a
robot. A robot car called Rover traveled to Mars.
The Rover's job was to collect facts about Mars.
The Rover picked up rocks. It took pictures. It
collected facts about the weather on Mars.

Things the Rover Did

TRY THIS

Make up your own title for the selection.

SCHOOL-HOME CONNECTION Read newspaper
captions with your child. Discuss the photos and
captions.

54

Practice Book
Gather Around • Lesson 7

© Harcourt

Name _____

► **Put the two word parts together. Double the last letter before you add <u>ed</u> or <u>ing</u>. Write the word to complete the sentence.**

stop + ed

_____

- - - - - - - - - - - - - - - - - - - -

1. The bus has _____ .

get + ing

_____

- - - - - - - - - - - - - - - - - - - -

2. Many people are _____ on.

put + ing

_____

- - - - - - - - - - - - - - - - - - - -

3. That man is _____

his big bag on the shelf.

drop + ed

_____

- - - - - - - - - - - - - - - - - - - -

4. Oh no! He _____ it!

step + ing

_____

- - - - - - - - - - - - - - - - - - - -

5. Who is _____ on my sneaker?

SCHOOL-HOME CONNECTION Ask your child to read aloud the sentences he or she completed. Take turns making up your own sentences with some of the words your child wrote.

55

Practice Book
Gather Around • Lesson 7

▶ **Read the words. Then read the name of each group. Write each word in the group where it belongs.**

Words With <u>ool</u>

_____
- - - - - - - - - - - -
_____
- - - - - - - - - - - -
_____
- - - - - - - - - - - -
_____

Words With <u>oot</u>

_____
- - - - - - - - - - - -
_____
- - - - - - - - - - - -
_____
- - - - - - - - - - - -
_____

Words With <u>ooth</u>

_____
- - - - - - - - - - - -
_____
- - - - - - - - - - - -
_____
- - - - - - - - - - - -
_____

Words Without <u>oo</u>

_____
- - - - - - - - - - - -
_____
- - - - - - - - - - - -
_____
- - - - - - - - - - - -
_____
- - - - - - - - - - - -
_____

Spelling Words

cool
tool
toot
tooth
booth
boot
read
head
carry
hours

SCHOOL-HOME CONNECTION Read the Spelling Words aloud, out of order, and have your child point to each word you say. Then take turns making up sentences using two or three of the words.

 56

© Harcourt

Name _____

► **Write the word from the box that names each picture.**

boots	broom	moon	spool	spoon	tools

1.

_____

- - - - - - - - - - - - - - - -

_____

2.

_____

- - - - - - - - - - - - - - - -

_____

3.

_____

- - - - - - - - - - - - - - - -

_____

4.

_____

- - - - - - - - - - - - - - - -

_____

5.

_____

- - - - - - - - - - - - - - - -

_____

6.

_____

- - - - - - - - - - - - - - - -

_____

© Harcourt

SCHOOL-HOME CONNECTION Have your child read aloud the words he or she wrote on this page. Then ask which two of those words rhyme.

57

Practice Book
Gather Around • Lesson 8

Name _____

▶ **Write the word that best completes each
sentence.**

isn't   don't   hasn't
_____

----

1. The spacecraft _____
   landed yet.

_____

aren't   isn't   don't
_____

----

2. We _____ have long
   to wait until we reach Mars.

_____

3. Mars has two moons, but they

don't   isn't   aren't
_____

_____ very big.

_____

don't   hasn't   doesn't
_____

----

4. Mars _____ have water.

TRY THIS Make two lists. Call one list "Things I Like" and the other
list "Things I Don't Like." Which list is longer?

 SCHOOL-HOME CONNECTION Work with
your child to think of sentences that use the
words *doesn't* and *don't*.

58

Practice Book
Gather Around • Lesson 8

© Harcourt

Name _____

▶ **Write the word from the box that best completes each sentence.**

| broom | food | noon | soon | spoon |

_____

1. It's almost _____.

_____

2. Our friends will be here _____.

_____

3. Bring the _____
so I can sweep.

_____

4. Is the _____ ready?

_____

5. Use this big _____ to stir it.

 SCHOOL-HOME CONNECTION Ask your child to read aloud the sentences she or he completed. Together, talk about things you might do at noon.

59

Practice Book
Gather Around • Lesson 8

© Harcourt

▶ **Write the word from the box that best completes each sentence.**

against	shook	fire	quietly	careful

_____

1. We made a _____ in our camp.

_____

2. We were _____
to make our fire safe.

_____

3. We sat _____ and watched it.

_____

4. I leaned _____ my dad.

_____

5. After a while, he _____ me awake.

SCHOOL-HOME CONNECTION Have your child read aloud the sentences he or she completed. Then ask your child to make up some original sentences using the words in the box.

60

© Harcourt

Name _____

▶ **Circle the word that names the picture.
Then write the word.**

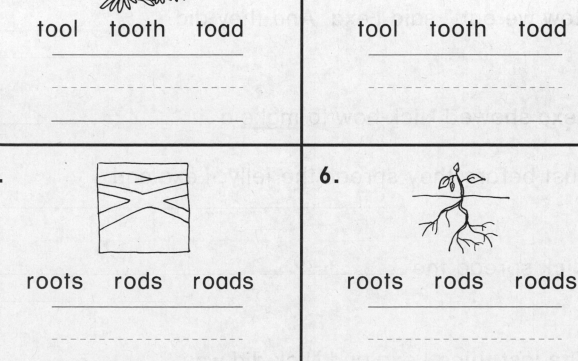

1.

boot   boat   bat

_____

- - - - - - - - - - - - - - - -

_____

2.

boot   boat   bat

_____

- - - - - - - - - - - - - - - -

_____

3.

tool   tooth   toad

_____

- - - - - - - - - - - - - - - -

_____

4.

tool   tooth   toad

_____

- - - - - - - - - - - - - - - -

_____

5.

roots   rods   roads

_____

- - - - - - - - - - - - - - - -

_____

6.

roots   rods   roads

_____

- - - - - - - - - - - - - - - -

_____

SCHOOL-HOME CONNECTION Have your child read aloud the word he or she wrote to name each picture. Then ask how your child knew that the other word choices did not fit the picture.

61

© Harcourt

Name _____

▶ **Read the story. Then finish the sentences
about the story.**

One day Nick went to play with his friend Lexa. "Do you
want to make a sandwich?" she asked him.

"First we need bread," she told
Nick. Nick and Lexa put bread on
their plates.

"Next we need peanut butter.
Spread the peanut butter on the
bread," said Lexa. They did.

"Now we need jelly," said Lexa. "Spread the jelly on the
peanut butter."

"It looks good," said Nick. "Now what?"

"Now we eat!" said Lexa. And they did.

_____

- -

1. Lexa showed Nick how to make a _____.

2. Just before they spread the jelly, Lexa and

_____

- -

Nick spread the _____.

_____

- - - - - - - - - - - - - - - - - - -

3. The last thing Lexa and Nick did was _____.

 SCHOOL-HOME CONNECTION Ask your
child to read the story aloud. Together, make
up a story about something else Lexa and
Nick might do.

 62

Practice Book
Gather Around • Lesson 8

© Harcourt

Name _____

▶ **Read the words in the box. Write the
word that completes each clue.**

boot	broom	hoot	room	root	zoom

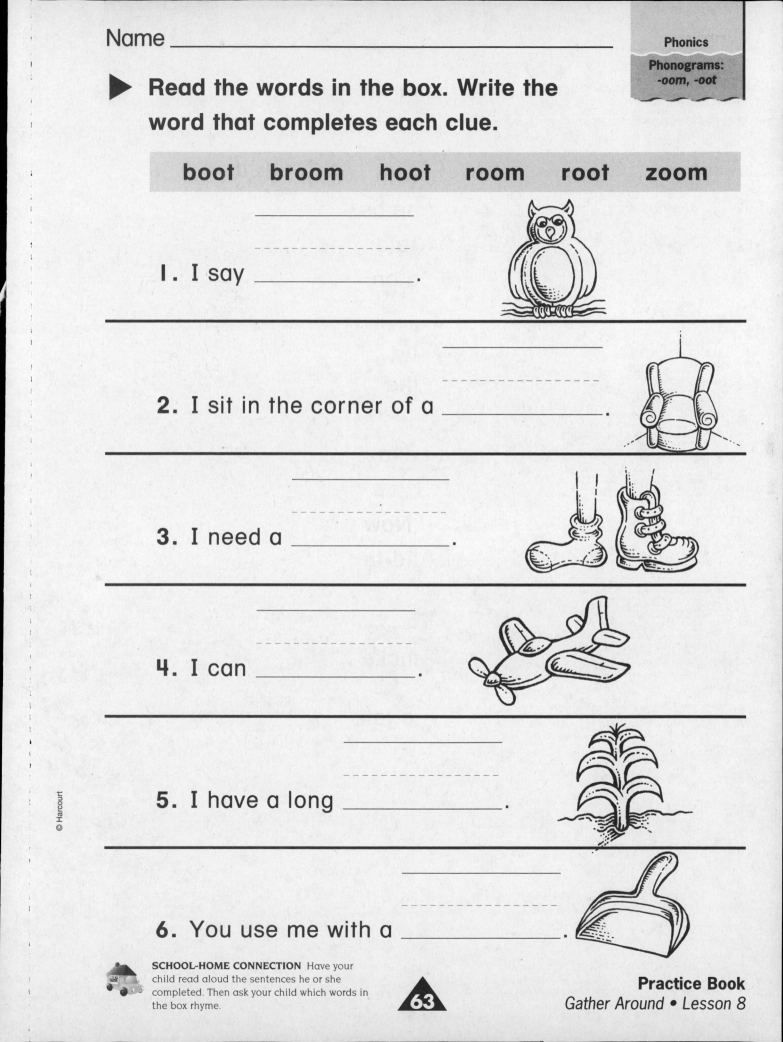

1. I say _____ .

2. I sit in the corner of a _____ .

3. I need a _____ .

4. I can _____ .

5. I have a long _____ .

6. You use me with a _____ .

SCHOOL-HOME CONNECTION Have your
child read aloud the sentences he or she
completed. Then ask your child which words in
the box rhyme.

63

Practice Book
Gather Around • Lesson 8

© Harcourt

Frog and Mouse

1

Fold

Fold

Mouse could not stay and play. He hurried off to work.

3

Then the two played near the woods.

8

"Make sure you get set for winter. Then you may play."

6

Practice Book
Gather Around • Cut-out Fold-up Book

4

Winter was near. Mouse did not want to be caught in the cold without a home.

2

One gray night Frog wanted to play with Mouse.

His father always said, "Son, find a winter home."

5

Frog helped Mouse until the job was finished.

Home

7

Find Something to Do

1

My tower crashes. My mom says, "Find something different to do."

3

© Harcourt

How do you find something to do?

8

Of course I want to help. This is something to do.

9

Practice Book
Gather Around • Cut-out Fold-up Book

2 During a rainstorm, my mom says, "Find something to do."

4 I run like a wild animal. My mom says, "Listen, child, you need to mind."

5 "Are you ready to help with these cookies?"

7 This cookie is big enough for both of us.

Fold

Fold

© Harcourt

Old Rover

1

"Do you want toast?" asked Jake.

3

Rover didn't stop. He ate the jam and toast. Now we will have to clean the floor!

8

Jake came in with the toast. Rover went to see.

9

4

"Yes, a piece of toast with jam, please," I said.

2

I was sick and in my bed. I had a bad cold.

Rover jumped up and pulled the blanket. I scolded him.

5

Rover sniffed and jumped all over the bed. "Stop!" I said.

7

The Bridge

1

Three goats went to cross the bridge. The little goat said they'd be okay.

3

"I'm sorry, Troll, but this rail is not safe," said the goat.

6

"Here's a page of notes. Don't budge until you fix this bridge," said the goat.

8

Fold

Fold

An angry troll made a pledge. "This is my bridge. No one will cross it."

Fold

Fold

4

"Stay off my bridge!" said the troll. "I'd better," said the goat. "You have a lot of work to do."

"Just look at this hole! I nearly fell. You should take better care of your bridge."

7

5

"You're kidding," said the troll. "Look at this edge," said the goat. "It needs paint."

Three Moles and a Mule

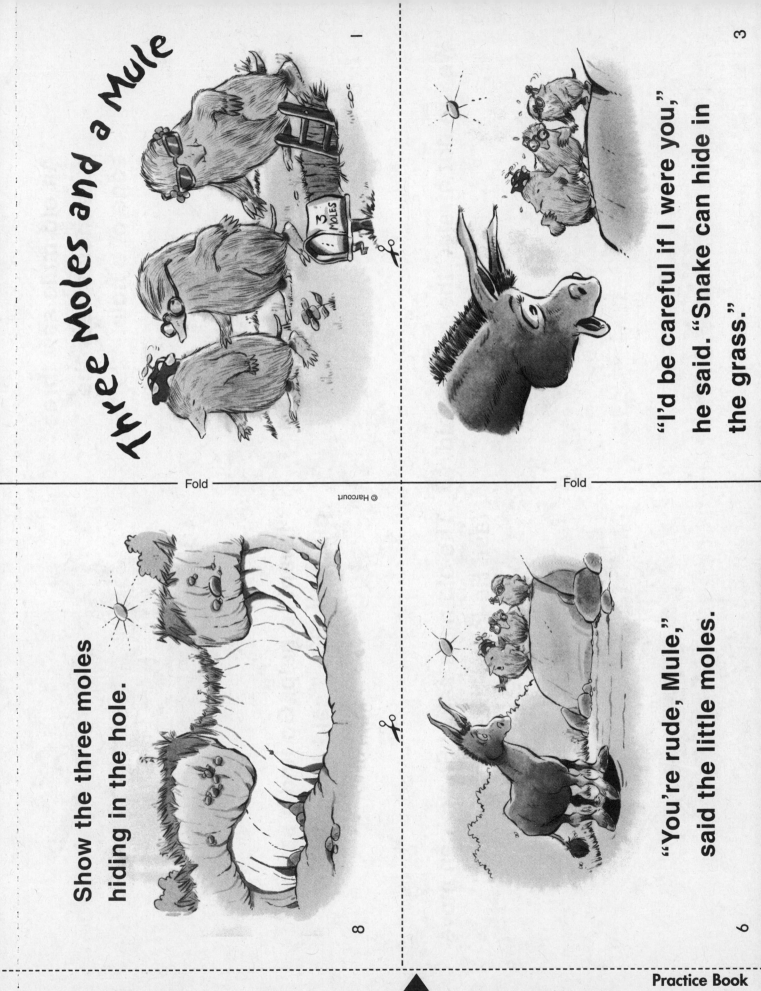

3

"I'd be careful if I were you,"
he said. "Snake can hide in
the grass."

Fold

Show the three moles
hiding in the hole.

8

"You're rude, Mule,"
said the little moles.

6

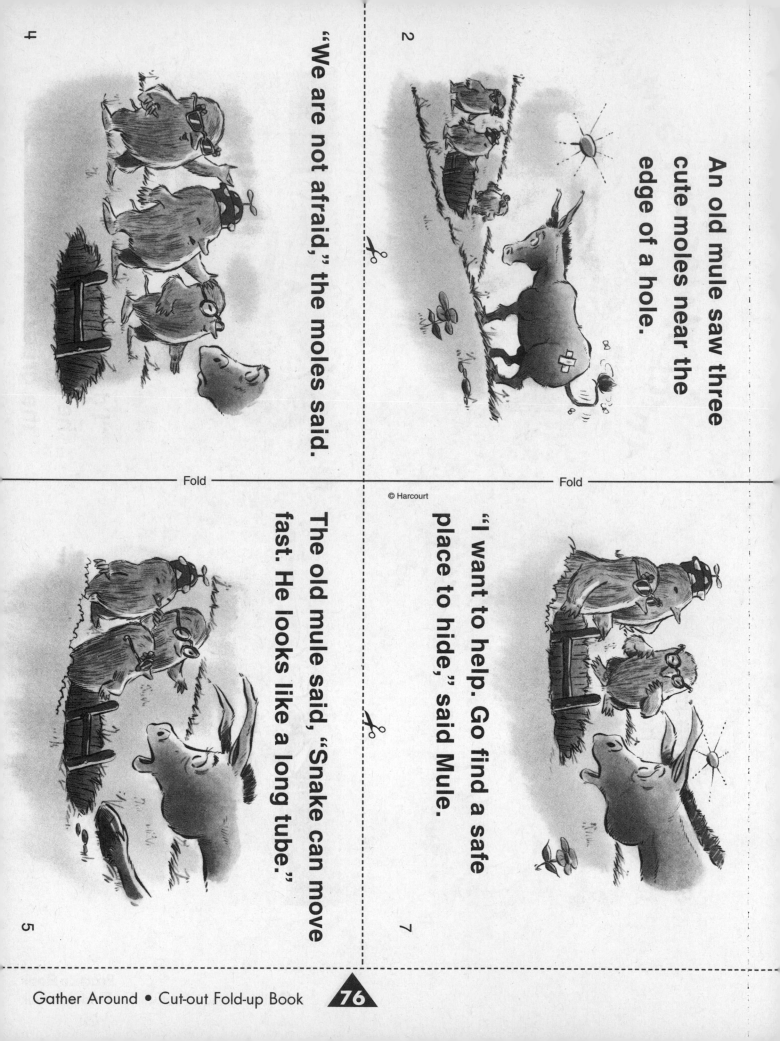

An old mule saw three cute moles near the edge of a hole.

"We are not afraid," the moles said.

— Fold —

— Fold —

© Harcourt

"I want to help. Go find a safe place to hide," said Mule.

The old mule said, "Snake can move fast. He looks like a long tube."

Ready for

Space

1

If I could, I'd leave right now and head for the stars.

3

© Harcourt

I'd wave to my parents on Earth.

8

When I got there, I'd get ready for a walk. What would I see?

6

I'd leave in the afternoon.

Sometimes I sit for hours and think about space.

— Fold —

© Harcourt

— Fold —

I wonder if I could bring my bicycle. No, not to space.

What could I carry back? What would I do?

ZOO RACE

1

The baboon soon led the way. 3

Fold

© Harcourt

Who do you think will win?

ZOO RACE

8

The crocodile moved quietly ahead of the others. 6

Fold

Practice Book
Gather Around • Cut-out Fold-up Book

The ostrich shook her feathers and ran against the wind.

2

Get ready. Get set. Go!

✂

Fold

© Harcourt

Fold

Don't be fooled by his size. The rhinoceros ran quickly over the mud.

Be careful, everyone. The gazelle is ahead now.

✂

Gather Around • Cut-out Fold-up Book

80

Skills and Strategies Index

81

Skills and Strategies Index

Phonograms
-ice, ide **L4** 46
-oom, -oot **L5** 63
-own, -ound **L4** 54

Short Vowels
/e/ea **L5** 49, 51

Vowel Variants
/ōō/oo **L5** 57, 59
/ou/ow, ou **L4** 48, 50

CVVC-CVVCC Words (with *ee, ea, ow, oa*) **L4** 13
CVC-CVCe Words (*a, a-e*) **L4** 21
CVCCy-CCVCCy Words **L4** 29
CVC-CVCe Words (with *i, i-e*) **L4** 37
CVC-CVCe Words (with *o, o-e*) **L4** 68
CVCe-CCVCe Words (with *ace, ice*) **L4** 45
CCVVC Words (with *ou, ow*) **L4** 52

CVVC and *–igh* Words **L5** 7
CVV-CVVC-CVCe Words (*ai, ay, a-e*) **L5** 15
CVCe-CVCC Words (with *i-e, i*) **L5** 22
CVCe-CVCC Words (with *o-e, o*) **L5** 30
CVCe-CVCCe Words (with *ge, dge*) **L5** 38
CVCe Words (with *u-e, a-e, i-e, o-e*) **L5** 46
CVC-CVVC Words (*e, ea*) **L5** 53
CVVC-CVVCC Words (*oo, oa*) **L5** 61

SPELLING
L4 8, 16, 24, 32, 40, 47, 55, 63
L5 2, 10, 17, 25, 33, 41, 48, 56

STUDY SKILL
Alphabetical Order **L4** 14, 38, 61

VOCABULARY
L4 12, 20, 28, 36, 44, 51, 59, 67
L5 6, 14, 21, 29, 37, 45, 52, 60

· TROPHIES ·

End-of-Selection Tests

Grade 1

Directions: Fill in the circle by the correct answer.

Sample   Do you have _____ pets?
○ always
○ almost
○ any

Vocabulary

1. The man _____ his cats to the vet.
○ that
○ care
○ took

2. My family has _____ cats.
○ eight
○ each
○ any

3. Dan will _____ for the dog.
○ only
○ care
○ could

© Harcourt

4. Mom is _____ with the baby.
- ○ busy
- ○ but
- ○ boots

5. _____ Martha Smith is a good vet.
- ○ By
- ○ Mr.
- ○ Dr.

Comprehension

6. Dr. Smith is a vet at the _____.
- ○ big house
- ○ animal shelter
- ○ old town

7. What does Dr. Smith do first each day?
- ○ meets a special cat
- ○ plays with the dogs
- ○ checks new animals

8. Muffin was a _____.
- ○ lost kitty
- ○ big dog
- ○ special food

© Harcourt

On the Job with Dr. Martha Smith

9. Why does Dr. Smith watch new animals when they come to the shelter?

○ to give them a bath

○ to see if they are healthy

○ to see how they act

Directions: Draw or write the answer to the question.

10. What are three kinds of animals that Dr. Smith gets at the shelter?

© Harcourt

Name _____ Date _____

Little Bear's Friend

© Harcourt

Directions: Fill in the circle by the correct answer.

Sample   Mom _____ the door for me.
   ○ only
   ○ opened
   ○ helped

Vocabulary

1. The bird sits _____ in the treetop.
   ○ high
   ○ how
   ○ hides

2. My friends always say _____ .
   ○ hold
   ○ here
   ○ hello

3. Little Bear _____ cookies.
   ○ listened
   ○ loved
   ○ walked

Practice Book
Time Together

4. Can we play together _____ soon?
- ○ again
- ○ also
- ○ above

5. The sea is a pretty _____.
- ○ red
- ○ busy
- ○ blue

Comprehension

6. Little Bear can not play with the squirrels because he has to _____.
- ○ climb the tree
- ○ go home for lunch
- ○ play with Emily

7. The little girl thinks she is _____.
- ○ funny
- ○ lost
- ○ busy

8. Emily wants Little Bear to _____.
- ○ go away
- ○ be her friend
- ○ eat lunch with her

© Harcourt

9. Where does Emily live?

◯ in a tree house

◯ in a big town

◯ by the river

Directions: Draw or write the answer to the question.

10. What does Little Bear see from the treetop?

_____

- -

_____

_____

- -

_____

Practice Book
Time Together

Directions: Fill in the circle by the correct answer.

Sample   We can pick _____ flowers.
  ◯ warm
  ◯ with
  ◯ wild

Vocabulary

1. The wild flowers grow in a _____.
  ◯ field
  ◯ follow
  ◯ family

2. Put _____ cookies in the bag.
  ◯ tall
  ◯ twelve
  ◯ young

3. They will _____ here for their friends.
  ◯ wait
  ◯ where
  ◯ way

4. Do you have _____ book?
- ◯ eight
- ◯ other
- ◯ another

5. Don't _____ the warm pan.
- ◯ took
- ◯ touch
- ◯ grow

Comprehension

6. What can the bee find in each flower?
- ◯ hive
- ◯ nectar
- ◯ honey

7. Busy Bee is a _____ bee.
- ◯ queen
- ◯ drone
- ◯ worker

8. Inside the hive, the bees make _____.
- ◯ eggs
- ◯ cells
- ◯ nectar

© Harcourt

9. Grubs change to bees in _____ days.

◯ four

◯ nine

◯ twelve

Directions: Draw or write the answer to the question.

10. What happens to grubs inside the cells?

Directions: Fill in the circle by the correct answer.

Sample The little bird _____ from the nest to the tree.
- ○ flew
- ○ walked
- ○ joined

Vocabulary

1. I _____ you had fed the animals.
- ○ talked
- ○ thought
- ○ touched

2. Do you _____ where the bird is?
- ○ took
- ○ would
- ○ wonder

3. Some birds are _____ of cats.
- ○ afraid
- ○ away
- ○ almost

4. There is _____ in the bag.
- ○ almost
- ○ nothing
- ○ night

5. The little bird will _____ to fly.
- ○ learn
- ○ listen
- ○ thought

Comprehension

6. While the other birds test their wings, the little blue bird watches because he is _____.
- ○ young
- ○ afraid
- ○ warm

7. When the blue bird wants to know what is out there, the mother bird says, "_____."
- ○ Many things
- ○ Anything
- ○ Nothing

8. Who does the little bird fly with first?
- ○ red bird
- ○ green bird
- ○ mother bird

The Story of a Blue Bird

9. Once the blue bird flies, he is not _____ .
- ○ sad
- ○ funny
- ○ afraid

Directions: Draw or write the answer to the question.

10. Who does the blue bird fly with at the end of the story?

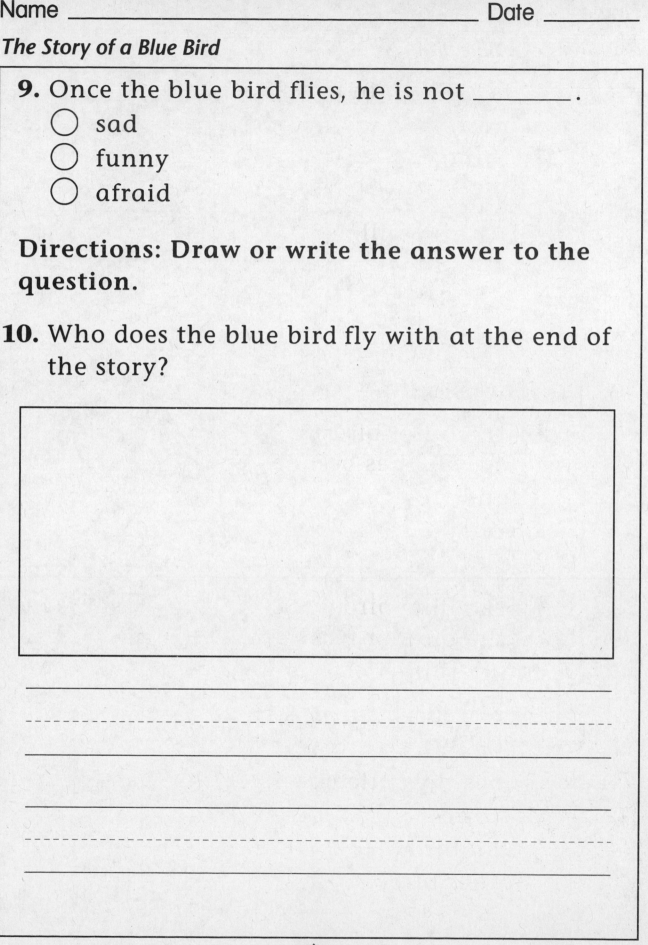

_____

- -

_____

_____

- -

_____

Practice Book
Gather Around

Directions: Fill in the circle by the correct answer.

Sample   They are wet because they were
              _____ in the rain.
              ○ caught
              ○ near
              ○ flew

Vocabulary

1. They _____ so they would not get too wet.
   ○ thought
   ○ hurried
   ○ happily

2. Their house is _____ the field.
   ○ about
   ○ over
   ○ near

3. Dan is the man's _____ .
   ○ sister
   ○ son
   ○ mom

Practice Book
Gather Around

4. Are you _____ it is raining?
- ○ sure
- ○ always
- ○ only

5. This is a _____, wet day.
- ○ water
- ○ old
- ○ cold

Comprehension

6. Toad stands by the stove _____.
- ○ to eat tea and cake
- ○ to dry his clothes
- ○ because the day is spoiled

7. A young frog is called a _____.
- ○ chick
- ○ pollywog
- ○ fish

8. Where does Frog's father tell him to look for spring?
- ○ around the corner
- ○ along the river
- ○ in the river

© Harcourt

9. When it stops raining, Frog and Toad _____.
- ○ find winter
- ○ find a worm
- ○ find spring

Directions: Draw or write the answer to the question.

10. When the rain stopped, Frog and Toad rushed outside. What do you think they found?

_____

- -

_____

_____

- -

_____

Practice Book
Gather Around

Directions: Fill in the circle by the correct answer.

Sample My friends grow _____ corn and flowers in their garden.
○ always
○ but
○ both

Vocabulary

1. Jan is _____ to go.
○ ready
○ almost
○ right

2. We don't play outside _____ the storm.
○ above
○ during
○ from

Comprehension

3. How many toes does a brown bear have?
○ five
○ four
○ two

4. Brown bears live near water so they can

_____ .

○ play tag
○ find food
○ stand up

5. Baby bears are called _____ .

○ chicks
○ pups
○ cubs

6. How is the walk of a brown bear different from other furry animals?

○ Brown bears walk on their toes.
○ Brown bears put their feet down flat.
○ Brown bears run and hop.

7. Brown bears eat _____ .

○ only fish
○ both plants and animals
○ only clams and salmon

8. How do bears get ready for winter?

○ They take a nap.
○ They eat a lot.
○ They make a den.

9. When bears hibernate, they are _____.
- ◯ very cold
- ◯ in a deep sleep
- ◯ fishing for food

Directions: Draw or write the answer to the question.

10. How many cubs does a mother bear usually have?

_____

- -

_____

_____

- -

_____

Practice Book
Gather Around

Directions: Fill in the circle by the correct answer.

Sample A _____ likes to find answers to questions.
- ○ diver
- ○ detective
- ○ teacher

Vocabulary

1. Look where you walk because the _____ is wet.
- ○ floor
- ○ whistle
- ○ house

2. Take that _____ of cake.
- ○ people
- ○ piece
- ○ day

3. It is fun to learn about _____.
- ○ nothing
- ○ helps
- ○ nature

© Harcourt

4. The bird _____ up a big worm.
- ○ feels
- ○ fills
- ○ pulls

5. Detectives look for _____.
- ○ friends
- ○ clues
- ○ toes

Comprehension

6. Where can a nature detective look for clues?
- ○ almost anywhere
- ○ only in the river
- ○ only in a tree

7. A cat does not leave claw marks because a cat _____.
- ○ does not have any claws
- ○ walks on only two of its paws
- ○ pulls its claws in when it walks

8. The tracks of a sea gull tell you _____.
- ○ where the wind was coming from
- ○ how old the gull is
- ○ when the gull was on the beach

© Harcourt

9. Gulls are like airplanes because they _____ .
  ○ take off at night
  ○ make funny sounds
  ○ take off facing the wind

Directions: Draw or write the answer to the question.

10. What is another place a nature detective can look for clues?

_____

- -

_____

- -

_____

Practice Book
Gather Around

Directions: Fill in the circle by the correct answer.

Sample   It is _____ time to go to bed.
  ○ fly
  ○ away
  ○ nearly

Vocabulary

1. Bob is _____ he can't find the book you want.
  ○ almost
  ○ pretty
  ○ sorry

2. It is _____ for you to sit here.
  ○ okay
  ○ once
  ○ over

3. Turtle got _____ when elephant splashed him.
  ○ tall
  ○ angry
  ○ young

© Harcourt

Practice Book
Gather Around

Comprehension

4. He asks his mother if he can _____.
- ○ play in the puddles
- ○ sail his boat in the puddles
- ○ sail his boat in the river

5. He put on _____ to go outside.
- ○ boots
- ○ a scarf
- ○ a smile

6. What does the alligator offer to do?
- ○ have tea with frog
- ○ get the boat back
- ○ swim with turtle

7. What does Pig do?
- ○ splash water
- ○ sail the boat
- ○ swim in the puddle

8. The _____ drank up the puddle.
- ○ elephant
- ○ alligator
- ○ turtle

© Harcourt

9. When the sun comes out, _____.

⃝ the animals play tag

⃝ the puddle dries up

⃝ the animals take the boat

Directions: Draw or write the answer to the question.

10. What is the story about?

_____

- -

_____

_____

- -

Practice Book
Gather Around

Directions: Fill in the circle by the correct answer.

Sample   The _____ is ten years old.
○ boy
○ man
○ saleslady

Vocabulary

1. They _____ a box of surprises to school.
○ listened
○ worked
○ brought

2. Here are a _____ flowers for you.
○ few
○ field
○ trees

3. Dan put a blue hat on his _____.
○ nose
○ head
○ foot

© Harcourt

A53

4. Have you _____ both story books?
○ read
○ answered
○ hurried

Comprehension

5. Poppleton wants a new bed because his
is _____ .
○ new
○ old
○ grown-up

6. The saleslady took Poppleton to try _____ .
○ four beds
○ the softest bed
○ the biggest bed

7. When the saleslady gets Poppleton a book,
he looks at _____ .
○ TV
○ the pictures
○ a few pages

8. Next, Poppleton wants _____ .
○ cookies
○ crackers
○ water

A54

© Harcourt

9. The last thing Poppleton asks for is _____.
  ◯ a game
  ◯ some food
  ◯ bluebirds

Directions: Draw or write the answer to the question.

10. Why do you think the saleslady says again and again, "Do you want the bed?"

© Harcourt

Directions: Fill in the circle by the correct answer.

Sample The baby takes a nap every _____ .
○ year
○ afternoon
○ hour

Vocabulary

1. My _____ will be home from work soon.
○ brain
○ thoughts
○ parents

2. You can ride my _____ .
○ bicycle
○ fish
○ bear

3. How many _____ do you sleep each night?
○ years
○ days
○ hours

Practice Book
Gather Around

Sleep Is for Everyone

4. We can _____ the box to the front door.
- ⭕ climb
- ⭕ carry
- ⭕ box

Comprehension

5. A chicken's eyelids are different from yours because they _____.
- ⭕ go up when they sleep
- ⭕ go down when they sleep
- ⭕ have no eyelids

6. How does an elephant sleep?
- ⭕ It sits down.
- ⭕ It stands up.
- ⭕ It curls up.

7. Young people need _____ sleep than grown-ups.
- ⭕ more
- ⭕ less
- ⭕ old

Practice Book
Gather Around

© Harcourt

8. Schoolchildren should have about _____ hours of sleep every night.
- ○ two to three
- ○ ten to twelve
- ○ five to eight

9. The only time your brain rests is when you are _____ .
- ○ asleep
- ○ awake
- ○ walking

Sleep Is for Everyone

Directions: Draw or write the answer to the question.

10. Give one reason why you need rest.

_____

- -

_____

- -

_____

Practice Book
Gather Around

© Harcourt

Baboon

Directions: Fill in the circle by the correct answer.

Sample The ground _____ when the elephants walked by.
- ○ should
- ○ took
- ○ shook

Vocabulary

1. Do not go near the hot _____ .
- ○ special
- ○ fire
- ○ flowers

2. Put my bicycle _____ the house.
- ○ against
- ○ almost
- ○ over

3. Dad did not want to wake us so he walked _____ .
- ○ always
- ○ happily
- ○ quietly

© Harcourt

4. Be _____ when you pick up the hot pan.
- ○ careful
- ○ angry
- ○ sorry

Comprehension

5. In the forest Baboon learned that some of the world is _____ .
- ○ blue
- ○ green
- ○ red

6. The turtle lets Baboon see the world can be _____ .
- ○ fast
- ○ soft
- ○ slow

7. When baboon saw the fire, his mother said _____ .
- ○ the world is always hot
- ○ the world is not always hot
- ○ be careful

© Harcourt

Practice Book
Gather Around

8. A hungry _____ might try to eat Baboon.

⭕ elephant

⭕ crocodile

⭕ monkey

9. Baboon was afraid of the _____.

⭕ elephants

⭕ gazelle

⭕ rhinoceros

Practice Book
Gather Around

Directions: Draw or write the answer to the question.

10. What does Baboon learn about the world from his mother?